GENDER EQUALITY

THE TIME HAS COME

IPS-NATHAN LECTURES

GENDER EQUALITY

THE TIME HAS COME

CORINNA LIM

Published by

World Scientific Publishing Co. Pte. Ltd.

5 Toh Tuck Link, Singapore 596224

USA office: 27 Warren Street, Suite 401-402, Hackensack, NJ 07601

UK office: 57 Shelton Street, Covent Garden, London WC2H 9HE

National Library Board, Singapore Cataloguing in Publication Data
Name(s): Lim, Corinna.
Title: Gender equality : the time has come / Corinna Lim.
Other Title(s): IPS-Nathan Lectures.
Description: Singapore : World Scientific Publishing Co. Pte Ltd., [2022] | Includes bibliography.
Identifier(s): ISBN 978-981-12-4868-9 (hardback) | 978-981-12-4934-1 (paperback) |
    978-981-12-4869-6 (ebook for institutions) | 978-981-12-4870-2 (ebook for individuals)
Subject(s): LCSH: Sex role--Singapore. | Women--Singapore--Social conditions. |
    Women--Singapore--Economic conditions. | Equality--Singapore.
Classification: DDC 305.42095957--dc23

British Library Cataloguing-in-Publication Data
A catalogue record for this book is available from the British Library.

For any available supplementary material, please visit
https://www.worldscientific.com/worldscibooks/10.1142/12596#t=suppl

Desk Editor: Lai Ann

Typeset by Stallion Press
Email: enquiries@stallionpress.com

THE S R NATHAN FELLOWSHIP FOR THE STUDY OF SINGAPORE

AND THE IPS-NATHAN LECTURE SERIES

The S R Nathan Fellowship for the Study of Singapore was established by the Institute of Policy Studies (IPS) in 2013 to support research on public policy and governance issues. With the generous contributions of individual and corporate donors, and a matching government grant, IPS raised around S$5.9 million to endow the Fellowship.

Each S R Nathan Fellow, appointed under the Fellowship, delivers a series of IPS-Nathan Lectures during his or her term. These public lectures aim to promote public understanding and discourse on issues of critical national interest.

The Fellowship is named after Singapore's sixth and longest-serving President, the late S R Nathan, in recognition of his lifetime of service to Singapore.

IPS-Nathan Lectures

Print ISSN: 2630-4996
Online ISSN: 2630-5003

CONTENTS

FOREWORD

I am very honoured and humbled to be the first civil society activist to be awarded the S R Nathan Fellowship.

Traditionally, this Fellowship has been awarded to eminent persons who have distinguished themselves in business, civil service or academic circles.

As someone who has spent close to half my life challenging the status quo to improve women's rights and gender equality in Singapore, I am delighted to be the one to break the above tradition, especially in 2021, a year which the Singapore government has designated as the "Year of Celebrating SG Women".

The most difficult preliminary task was to decide on the topics that could be covered in the three one-hour long lectures.

You may wonder, is there really so much to say about gender equality in Singapore?

Yes, there is. In my work at the Association of Women for Action and Research (AWARE) for the last 30 years as a volunteer and as AWARE's

Executive Director, I hear heartbreaking stories about women almost every day: women who have been denied jobs because they are pregnant or return to jobs after their pregnancy to find a notice of termination on their desk; women traumatised by sexual violence and who struggle to get through the justice system to ensure that no one else suffers the same fate; lower-income mothers who are denied support because of their migrant or marital status; women who after joining our support groups, left their abusive relationships when they realised they were not alone and had the power to change their lives.

Their challenges are not just personal or interpersonal, but are often caused, exacerbated or compounded by systemic factors — laws, policies, practices and sexist values and beliefs. Often, they intersect with issues of race, religion, class, sexuality and marital status.

Even as we have seen many improvements in the status and rights of women, there is still a long way to go — from ending gender violence, discrimination and prejudice in all its forms; to challenging traditional gender norms and stereotypes that hinder women and men from achieving their full potential and contribute to the dearth of women in leadership and persistent gender pay gaps; and supporting groups of marginalised women such as unwed or low-income mothers and migrant spouses.

So I took some leave from the trenches, to get a 50,000-foot perspective of where Singapore was, in terms of gender equality, what the key drivers and barriers are, and which are the most urgent to tackle, to accelerate our progress.

It boils down to the following four things that I deal with in the Lectures:

Lecture I — Herstory: The Road to Equality

    a)   Lessons from history: gender equality was never regarded or cultivated as a fundamental value by our founding fathers. Educating and empowering women were essential to build Singapore's economy and to win elections. But patriarchy ruled the day and was not regarded by our political leaders as something that could be changed. These early directions set the trajectory and limitations on how gender equality progressed in Singapore.

Lecture II — The Caring Economy

b) Family caregiving has generally been regarded as women's work, both in our families and by policymakers. Women are given four months of maternity leave and men two weeks of paternity leave.

Further, unpaid care work is overlooked and undervalued in our capitalist system. Singapore under-invests in caregiving support as policymakers expect (unpaid) female caregivers and (lowly paid) domestic workers to take care of the young and old.

We need to ramp up investments especially in providing support for caregiving for older persons, as caregiving needs will increase sharply with Singapore's rapidly ageing population.

Lecture III — Reset: Men, Women, Violence

c) Most efforts to promote gender equality have focused on women — women's development and empowerment. For too long, we have ignored the need to change societal norms that impose very restrictive norms of masculinity, including harmful ideas of male domination over other men and women. Many of these masculine norms are also harmful to men, leading to high rates of suicide and male violence.

d) Today's youth live in a highly sexualised world. They are exposed to sexting and online porn at an early age. Parents and educators lag behind and are not providing youths with the sexuality education and support they need to safely navigate the current environment. The unrealistic focus on "abstinence till marriage" results in young people turning to porn for their sex education and being exposed to sexual violence, rather than respect and consent in sexual interactions.

In these lectures, I have made many recommendations on how we can tackle each of the key issues that I have highlighted.

Most of these are not easy solutions, like changing the National Pledge and Constitution to establish gender equality as a fundamental value in our society; investing significantly more money in supporting our people's caregiving needs; and reviewing institutions like National Service to ensure that they do not contribute to masculine norms that are harmful.

But then again, we should ask ourselves: can we afford not to address gender equality when human talent is the only natural resource that Singapore has?

In fact, the question should be why Singapore did not pay more attention to this issue earlier, before our total fertility rates sunk to an abysmally low 1.1 births per woman. The low birth rate in turn has caused Singapore to be one of the fastest-ageing countries in the world. As the Nordic countries have shown, gender equality and substantial support for caregiving make for happier and larger families, thriving economies and high standards of living.

Technology has presented new challenges for the younger population by making porn widely available to young people and enabling the commission of sexual violations. Technology-facilitated sexual assault has been on AWARE's radar for the last few years and continues to rise. Women in Singapore are generally safe on the streets but less safe on the Internet.

The time has come — to reset the trajectory of gender equality in Singapore.

These lectures were well-timed by IPS to coincide with the government's review of gender equality in 2021. This review involves an extensive series of public dialogues titled "Conversations on Singapore Women's Development" which will culminate in a White Paper on making gender equality a fundamental value in Singapore.

Mr K Shanmugam, Minister for Home Affairs and Minister for Law, in announcing the public dialogues, said:

> *The idea of gender equality, should it not be imprinted deeply into our collective consciousness?*
> *The answer must be yes.*[1]

These lectures are my humble contribution to the current government review and beyond. It is my ardent hope that the current review will reset and improve the trajectory for gender equality in Singapore.

A big thank you to IPS, and especially to its director, Janadas Devan, for awarding me the prestigious S R Nathan Fellowship and giving me the opportunity to speak about ideals and aspirations that are fundamentally important to Singaporeans — justice, equality, respect, safety, living our best lives, regardless of gender, and care for our families and community.

My deepest gratitude to my research assistant, Fiachra MacFadden, who provided me with invaluable historical inputs and insights as a male feminist.

It has taken a village to write and deliver these lectures. I am blessed to have received helpful inputs and emotional support from my friends and colleagues. Robin, Shailey, Margie, Kani and Rebecca — I really could not have done these lectures without all of you.

I hope that my very presence as a Fellow and the content of these lectures will facilitate more discussions and accelerate the building of bridges between civil society and policymakers.

As Professor Chan Heng Chee said in her final lecture as the 7th S R Nathan Fellow:

> *The recent COVID-19 pandemic shows that civil society organisations have a role to play as an early warning system for social issues and fissures in society, be it the plight of abused women, the ageing poor, or foreign workers, no matter how*

---

[1] Ministry of Home Affairs, "Conversations on Women Development — Speech by K Shanmugam, Minister for Home Affairs and Minister for Law," September 20, 2020, https://www.mha.gov.sg/mediaroom/speeches/conversations-on-women-development-speech-by-mr-k-shanmugam-minister-for-home-affairs-and-minister-for-law.

unwelcome the feedback. The government and these organisations can work closer together as both are interested in improving the lives of the vulnerable to build a better community.[2]

Corinna Lim

27 July 2021

---

[2] Heng Chee Chan, *World in Transition: Singapore's Future* (Singapore: World Scientific, 2021), 88.

ABOUT THE MODERATORS

Kanwaljit Soin is a practising surgeon and was Singapore's first female Nominated Member of Parliament (1992–1996). She is the founder of many civil society organisations, including Women's Initiative for Ageing Successfully (WINGS) and the Association of Women for Action and Research (AWARE). For her work towards improving the lives of women, she was named Singapore's "Her World Woman of the Year" in 1992, and was inducted to the Singapore Women's Hall of Fame in 2014.

Lin Suling is Executive Editor at CNA, where she oversees its award-winning Commentary and Podcasts section and leads a team who works with opinion shapers and experts to define and discuss the most consequential news of the day — on Singapore, the Asia-Pacific and the world. She is also host of CNA's weekly "Heart of the Matter" podcast, which dives into the biggest news stories and hot-button issues with newsmakers to gain deep insights and figure what is at stake.

Eunice Olsen is Founder of Eunice Olsen Media and a former Nominated Member of Parliament in Singapore (2004–2009). She is recognised for her work in the media across Asia as a renowned speaker, host and advocate for women's empowerment. A Young Global Leader at the World Economic Forum, Eunice was conferred the ASEAN and Singapore Youth Awards. She is the creator of WomenTalk.com, a programme that celebrates extraordinary everyday women.

ABOUT THE COVER ILLUSTRATOR

Huang Minxian (emmecks.com) is a designer from Singapore. She graduated from the National University of Singapore in 2019, majoring in Industrial Design, and is currently working at the Institute of Policy Studies. She enjoys baking and hopes to open her own café one day.

Lecture I

HERSTORY: THE ROAD TO EQUALITY

Introduction

Let us start with some basic definitions to ensure that we are all on the same page. First, what is gender equality? Let us take the United Nations (UN) definitions, which are authoritative and clear: Gender equality refers to the equal rights, responsibilities and opportunities of women and men, girls and boys, to enable everyone to fulfil their potential.[1] Gender equality does not mean that women and men are the same, but that women's and men's rights, responsibilities and opportunities will not depend on whether they are born male or female.[2]

When we talk about gender equality, what aspects of gender equality are we talking about? For our discussion, I will be touching on six core dimensions of gender equality:

---

[1] UNICEF, "Gender Equality," accessed May 10, 2021, https://www.unicef.org/gender-equality; UN Women, "Concepts and Definitions," accessed May 10, 2021, https://www.un.org/womenwatch/osagi/conceptsandefinitions.htm.

[2] The UN also makes a distinction between sex and gender. Sex refers to the biological differences between male and female, for example, in terms of chromosomes, sex organs and hormones. Gender, on the other hand, is a social construct. Girls are generally socialised to be nurturing and boys are generally socialised to be ambitious and more aggressive. But these are not biologically predetermined.

- Equal education
- Economic equality
- Equal division of power and influence
- Equal distribution of unpaid housework and provision of care
- Equal health
- End of men's violence against women

This is the gender equality flower. It has six petals, each representing a key dimension of equality. At the heart of the flower are gender norms, beliefs and stereotypes — ideas such as "men are natural leaders" and "assertive women are bossy".

To address any one of these dimensions, we must deal with the beliefs and norms that affect that area. Let us take education, represented by the orange petal (Figure 1). If a government offers girls and boys equal access

Figure 1.   Gender equality flower

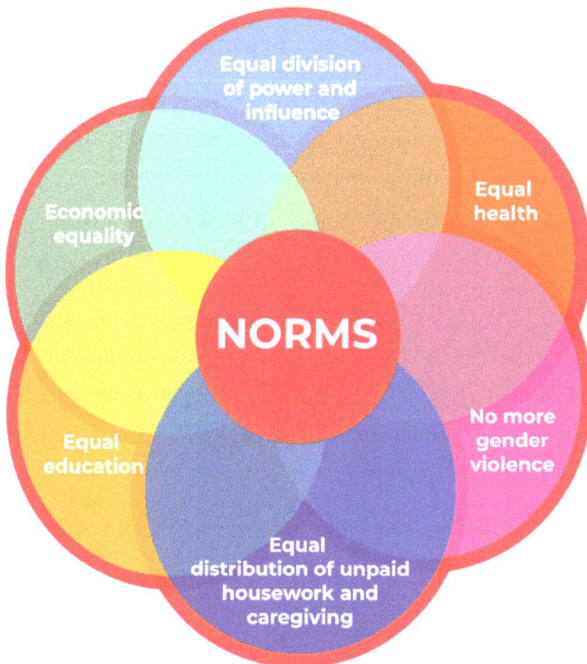

Source: Mithalina Taib for the Institute of Policy Studies

to education but parents believe that it is more important for their sons to be educated, equal education may not happen.

These dimensions are also linked to one another. For example, the blue petal, caregiving, is linked to the green and light blue petals, economic equality and leadership. If women are the primary caregivers at home, then they may have to short-change their career and leadership aspirations. Because the six dimensions are all linked, we have to work at all six. A weakness in any one dimension will stop the flower from blooming. Where there are equal opportunities in all areas, we will in turn see equal results — fairly equal numbers of men and women in leadership, in the workforce and as caregivers.[3]

Now that we have set the scene, let us see how Singapore fares in these different dimensions of gender equality. When we talk about this, we need to look at where we are today, compared to the past, as well as how each of the gender equality dimensions compare to one another.

Singapore on the World Economic Forum's Gender Gap Index

I would like to refer to the World Economic Forum's (WEF) 2021 Gender Gap Index (Figure 2).[4] The Index was created in 2006 and is updated every year.

Overall, Singapore is ranked 54th out of 156 countries, which does not sound great. But let us not get too hung up about the ranking. There are many different indices. The actual ranking should be taken with a pinch of salt. The WEF Index ranks us worse than others; in the UN Index, however, we are 12th. The disparity is large and depends on what is measured.

What I can say for sure is that Singapore is generally not in the top 10. It is the Nordic countries that consistently take the top spots. What is

---

[3] CEDAW Committee, "General Recommendation No. 25, on Article 4, Paragraph 1, of the Convention on the Elimination of All Forms of Discrimination Against Women, on Temporary Special Measures," Thirtieth Session, 2004, accessed June 6, 2021, https://www.un.org/womenwatch/daw/cedaw/recommendations/General%20 recommendation%2025%20(English).pdf.

[4] World Economic Forum, "Global Gender Gap Report 2021," accessed May 18, 2021, https://www.weforum.org/ reports/global-gender-gap-report-2021, 343.

Figure 2.   Global gender gap index for Singapore

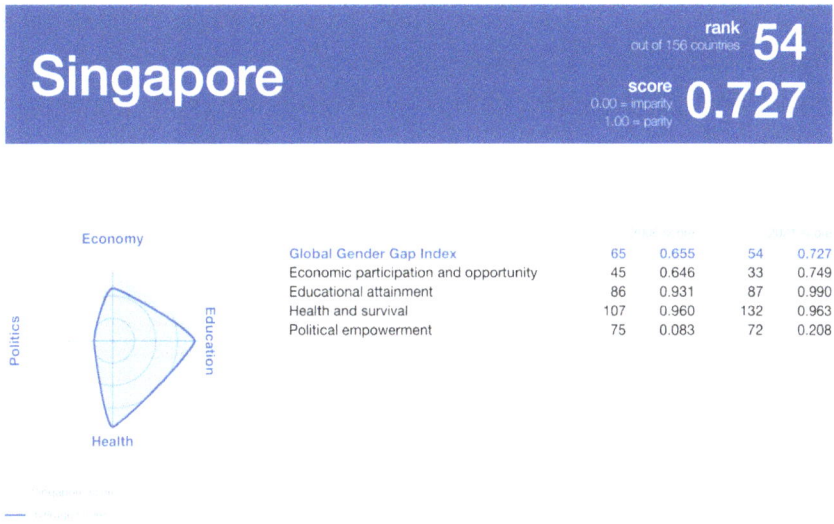

Singapore		rank out of 156 countries	**54**	
		score 0.00 = imparity 1.00 = parity	**0.727**	

Global Gender Gap Index	65	0.655	54	0.727
Economic participation and opportunity	45	0.646	33	0.749
Educational attainment	86	0.931	87	0.990
Health and survival	107	0.960	132	0.963
Political empowerment	75	0.083	72	0.208

Source: World Economic Forum, "Global Gender Gap Report 2021," accessed May 18, 2021, https://www.weforum.org/reports/global-gender-gap-report-2021, 343.

useful about the WEF assessment is that it indicates the relative strengths of each country's gender equality dimensions and how close they are to parity.

As you can see, the WEF Index covers four out of six of our gender equality dimensions — education, economy, politics and health. The outermost circle indicates gender parity. For education and health, Singapore is close to gender parity. For the economy, Singapore still has some ways to go. When it comes to political representation, we are even further behind. With only three women out of 20 ministers in the Cabinet (15 per cent), this is not surprising. The WEF does not include "family equality" and "men's violence against women". But this simple assessment gives a pretty good idea of where Singapore is in relation to different aspects of gender equality and should accord with most people's expectations.

Singapore Today, Compared with the Past

The development of Singapore since its independence is, as Peter Ho said in his S R Nathan lectures, "without precedent, and nothing short of a modern miracle".[5] Women have both benefited from this as well as played a critical role in Singapore's rapid modernisation and growth. The education and empowerment of women formed an essential part of Singapore's nation-building strategy. As founding Prime Minister Lee Kuan Yew said in 1975, "Societies which do not educate and use half their potential because they are women are those which will be the worse off."[6]

The impressive record of Singapore women's development speaks for itself:

- Women's literacy rate rose significantly from a mere 34 per cent in 1957 to 96 per cent in the year 2019.[7]
- Female labour force participation rate rose from below 20 per cent in 1957 to 61 per cent today.[8]
- Today, the female labour force is more highly educated than the male labour force because girls have outpaced boys in education.[9]
- Forty-one per cent of women in the labour force are degree holders, whereas 37 per cent of men in the labour force are degree holders.[10]

---

[5] Peter Ho, *The Challenges of Governance in a Complex World* (Singapore: World Scientific, 2017), 78.

[6] "Speech by the Prime Minister, Mr Lee Kuan Yew, at the NTUC's International Women's Year Seminar cum Exhibition at the DBS Auditorium on Monday, 1 September, 1975," National Archives of Singapore, accessed May 18, 2021, https://www.nas.gov.sg/archivesonline/data/pdfdoc/lky19750901.pdf.

[7] Kho Ee Moi, "Economic Pragmatism and the 'Schooling' of Girls in Singapore," *HSSE Online* 4, no. 2 (October 2015); Singapore Department of Statistics, "Education, Language Spoken and Literacy," [2019 data], accessed May 18, 2021, https://www.singstat.gov.sg/find-data/search-by-theme/population/education-language-spoken-and-literacy/latest-data.

[8] Seng Chew Chua and Singapore Department of Statistics, *State of Singapore, Report on the Census of Population: 1957* (Singapore: Government Printer, 1964); Ministry of Manpower and Singapore Department of Statistics, "Labour, Employment, Wages and Productivity," [2020 data], accessed April 28, 2021, https://www.tablebuilder.singstat.gov.sg/publicfacing/createDataTable.action?refId=12374.

[9] Ministry of Manpower, Manpower Research and Statistics Department, "Labour Force," [2020 data], accessed April 28, 2021, https://stats.mom.gov.sg/Pages/LabourForceTimeSeries.aspx.

[10] Ibid.

The Story So Far: Gender Equality in Singapore

How did we get to where we are today? Many of us have read and watched movies about the suffragettes and the various women's liberation movements in the West. But how many of us know the Singapore Story?

We owe a huge debt to the activists who fought for women in Singapore to be treated more fairly and to be safe from violence. For this reason alone, it is important to tell their stories.

The stories are also insightful. Since the gender equality review was announced, people have asked me: "How committed is Singapore to achieving gender equality? Why are they doing the gender equality review now to make gender equality a fundamental value? Does that mean it was never a fundamental value? How then are Singapore women so empowered and educated?"

These are great questions. The lessons from the past help us answer some of these questions. They also serve as a guide on what we can do to advance gender equality in Singapore.

Singapore Herstory

In terms of gender equality progress, we can roughly break our women's movement history — which I shall call "herstory" — down into four phases:

1) The Merdeka Period
2) The Men's Years
3) The Women Return Period
4) Ground-Up Activism

The Merdeka Period (1952–1970)

The Merdeka is where we see the first breakthrough for women's rights in Singapore that led to the enactment of the Women's Charter, policies for equal education for girls, and higher numbers of women in the labour force. This period is also an important part of Singapore's road to independence and the People's Action Party's (PAP) story of how it came into power in the 1960s. The main protagonists in this period are:

- The Singapore Council of Women (SCW) led by Shirin Fozdar and other women activists;
- The PAP Women's League, led by Chan Choy Siong and Ho Puay Choo.

Let me set the stage. It is post–World War II and the population stands at 1 million persons — this is double Singapore's pre-war population. People are mainly crammed into shophouses in the city area or shanty towns. Living conditions are deplorable.[11] Women emerge from the Japanese occupation eager to contribute to rebuilding Singapore society. They come forward to operate feeding centres and other welfare services.[12]

Women also rally to the call for decolonisation. For the first time, they join political parties and stand for elections. There are female representatives both in the Municipal and Legislative Councils. It is indeed an exciting time. We see a mushrooming of women's groups. There are community service clubs such as the Chinese Ladies' Association, work groups like the Singapore Nurses Association and religiously inspired groups like the Young Women's Christian Association. Their focus is on service, welfare, networking and recreation, not women's rights.[13]

This changes in 1952 when Shirin Fozdar brings together the leaders of the key women's groups to form the SCW to fight for women's rights. Shirin Fozdar hailed from India. She was an anti-colonial nationalist and a firebrand. Fierce and tireless. The SCW is led by a multiracial group consisting of women mainly in their 40s and 50s. They include notable names like Elizabeth Choy, Mrs George Lee, Mrs Seow Peck Leng, Checha

---

[11] Mark Ravinder Frost and Yu-Mei Balasingamchow, *Singapore: A Biography* (Singapore: Editions Didier Millet, 2012), 335.

[12] Phyllis Ghim-Lian Chew, "The Singapore Council of Women and the Women's Movement," *Journal of Southeast Asian Studies* 25, no. 1 (1994), 113.

[13] Ibid., 113–14.

Davis, Che Zahara Binte Noor Mohamed, Vilasini Menon and of course, Shirin Fozdar.

The SCW decides to focus their energy on a single issue: abolishing polygamy. Polygamy was rife in those times. Husbands set up multiple families that they had no means to support. Secondary wives and families were poorly treated and often abandoned by their husbands. The SCW actively lobbies the government, community groups and leaders on the polygamy issue for many years. Finally, it trains its focus on local political parties, who become more influential as Singapore gears up for self-government.

Of all the political parties, the PAP takes the strongest stand on women's rights. Why? For three reasons:

1)   PAP's socialist ideology
2)   Pressure from the PAP Women's League
3)   Strategy to win the women's vote

Let me elaborate on each of these points.

First Reason: PAP's Socialist Ideology

The early PAP had strong socialist leanings. Its 1959 political manifesto, *The Tasks Ahead*, sets out its position on women's rights:

> *In a full socialist society, for which the PAP will work for, all people will have equal rights and opportunities, irrespective of sex, race or religion. There is no place in a socialist society for exploitation of women. The PAP believes in the principle of equal pay for equal work.*[14]

The call to abolish polygamy is in line with PAP's socialist ideology.

---

[14] PAP, "Women in the New Singapore," in *The Tasks Ahead Part 2: PAP's Five-year Plan, 1959–1964* (Singapore: Petir, 1959), 17.

Second Reason: Pressure from the PAP's Women League

The other protagonist in the Merdeka Period, the PAP Women's League, plays an important role within the Party to push for women's rights. The Women's League (which is similar to the PAP Women's Wing today) is made up of women who are mainly Chinese-educated. The leader of the Women's League is a very capable politician, Chan Choy Siong, and her comrade, Ho Puay Choo.

Chan is Chinese-educated, the daughter of a *chee cheong fun* hawker. She is only 23 when she joins the PAP. Between studies, Chan Choy Siong helps out at her father's stall. She sees hawkers, like her father, victimised by corrupt city council officials. She develops a strong desire to eradicate corruption and improve the living conditions of people in Chinatown. Chan's husband, Ong Pang Boon, the former Minister for Labour, recalls how determined Chan was in the Party:

> *She took every opportunity at party meetings, conferences, in Parliament and mass rallies, to campaign for women's rights. When the PAP won the elections in 1959 and formed the first PAP Government, she was constantly pressing for the government to carry out the manifesto.*[15]

Chan Choy Siong, Ho Puay Choo and a third Women's League member, Oh Su Chen, are elected to the PAP's Central Executive Committee (CEC). They form three out of the 12 CEC members (25 per cent) and they drive the PAP's women's agenda to end polygamy and ensure equality of women with men.

The growing number of voices demanding for women's rights are part of a larger anti-colonial struggle for democracy and equal rights. This was

---

[15] Melanie Chew, *Leaders of Singapore* (Singapore: Resource Press, 1996), 177.

best illustrated in a radio broadcast given by Chan Choy Siong in 1960 where she said:

> *We must unite the strength of the women in the fight for a democratic, independent, non-communist and united socialist society. Only when this target is achieved can the women be said to be completely liberated.*[16]

In other words, if women's liberation is not achieved, then neither is real democracy and equality.

Third Reason: Strategy to Win the Women's Vote

The final and perhaps the most important reason for the PAP's pro-women position is political. The 1959 elections is the first time that voting is compulsory. Before this, few women voted. The PAP, calculating that the women's votes would be critical, decide to include women's emancipation as part of its election manifesto. As Lee Kuan Yew later remarked in his memoirs, this strategy and the inclusion of five female candidates in the landmark election were effective to distinguish the PAP from other parties.[17]

The PAP's strategy pays off. They win a landslide victory. Lee Kuan Yew is elected as Singapore's first Prime Minister. A total of five women are elected, four from PAP and one from an opposition party.

Women are given equal education. The government divides schools into morning and afternoon sessions to double the capacity of schools to take in girls. Women start going out to work in droves. The SCW presses the PAP to fulfil its promise of ending polygamy after the elections. The PAP lives up to this promise by introducing the Women's Charter.

---

[16] Quoted in Phyllis Chew, Jenny Lin Lam, Singapore Council of Women's Organisations, and Singapore Baha'i Women's Committee, *Voices & Choices: The Women's Movement in Singapore* (Singapore: Singapore Council of Women's Organisations and Singapore Baha'i Women's Committee, 1993), 85.

[17] Lee Kuan Yew, *The Singapore Story: Memoirs of Lee Kuan Yew* (Singapore Press Holdings, 1998), 325–26.

One thing to note: The PAP did not include gender equality in the Constitution or Pledge, unlike its reference to equality regardless of "race, language or religion". We will return to this point later.

The Women's Charter

Let me say a few words about the Women's Charter. The Women's Charter is one of the most progressive laws on women's rights to have ever been enacted in Southeast Asia. At that time, it was considered revolutionary. Not just because it outlawed polygamy but also because it did away with the English doctrine of coverture, which stripped women of their rights to sign contracts and own property when they got married. In speaking up for the Bill, Chan Choy Siong did not mince her words. She said:

> *Women in our society are like pieces of meat put on the table for men to slice. The PAP Government has made a promise. We cannot allow this inequality in the family to exist in this country. We will liberate women from the hands of the oppressor. With the passing of this legislation, women can contribute their part to the country.*[18]

The Women's Charter was passed in the Legislative Assembly on 24 May 1961. The female MPs saw the Charter as the first step towards equality. We celebrate the 60th Anniversary of the Women's Charter on 24 May 2021. This is also the date that I've picked for my third and final lecture. I hope you will join me for this lecture. Together, we can all toast our drink to the brave women, Shirin Fozdar, Chan Choy Siong, Ho Puay Choo and many others who set the rights of Singapore women off to a very good start.

Lessons Learnt

There are three lessons to be learnt from the Merdeka Period:

First, that women activists in politics and civil society play a critical role in advancing women's rights and gender equality. The early wins were

---

[18] Choy Siong Chan, speech given to the First Parliament on the Women's Charter Bill, April 6, 1960, *Hansard Parliamentary Debates* 12 (1960): 443.

only possible because of the relentless lobbying by female PAP activists and the SWC. The SWC initiated the Women's Charter and lobbied for about 10 years to achieve its goal to outlaw polygamy. Major change takes time and persistence. So it is important to have activists and groups that can carry out sustained advocacy, in and outside government.

Our early women's movement is often neglected in the telling of the Singapore Story. How many Singaporeans today are aware of the formidable local women's movement of the 1950s and 1960s? Many do not know this history.

The second lesson we can learn from this is that women voters have power. The PAP played their cards right in the 1959 elections to court new female voters. Fast-forward to the 2020 General Election where we saw the emergence of more female candidates in all parties and manifestos that included gender issues in a significant way.

Post-elections, we see parties setting up women's wings and launching initiatives that specifically target women. This trend will likely continue in an increasingly competitive political climate. Parties that pay attention to and understand women's needs, and explicitly adopt positions that support these needs, will find favour with female voters.

The third lesson is that equal opportunities for women to be educated and work are key to their liberation. Without this, we cannot even begin to talk about gender equality. In this respect, the PAP's economic pragmatism served women well. Educating women was both good for the economy and essential to women's development.

The empowerment of women in the early 1960s became really important when Singapore was ejected from the Federation of Malaysia in 1965. At that point, with human capital as its only asset, women's participation in the economy was critical to Singapore's survival. If the story ended here, you might think that this is a pretty good women's liberation story.

Unfortunately, the trajectory of the Merdeka Period did not continue in the next chapter of Herstory. In this next period, from 1971 to the early

1980s, we see what happens when the Men in White lead the way, without any women in the Party. I am calling this period "The Men's Years".

The Men's Years (1971–1983)

With the passing of the Women's Charter, the SCW lost its sense of mission. Shirin Fozdar left Singapore in 1961. Support for the SCW dwindled and it was deregistered in 1971. On the PAP's side, the big split in the PAP where many Members of Parliament (MPs) left the PAP to join the Barisan Sosialis caused the PAP to lose half of its female MPs. Chan Choy Siong retired from politics in 1970, leaving an all-male Parliament. The Women's League was dissolved in 1975. Parliament would not see another female MP for 14 years until 1984.

Without the moderating influence of the women politicians, we see the unfiltered patriarchal instincts of the all-male Parliament and Cabinet coming to the fore. It was during this period that we saw the enactment of the most sexist policies in the PAP's history. These policies adversely affected girls, women and families, and served to reinforce rather than dismantle patriarchal values. Thankfully, all of these have since been reversed but not before they left their mark on society. Let us have a look at two policies that were passed during the Men's Years.

Policy 1: Quota on Female Medical Students

In 1979, a policy was introduced to limit the number of female medical students to one-third of every cohort. The government considered medical education for women a poor return on investment. It felt that many female doctors would leave the profession to have babies upon marriage. Dr Toh Chin Chye, the Health Minister, also said in Parliament that it was very difficult for a woman to be a good doctor because "she had to be a wife and a mother besides performing night duty in government hospitals."[19] The

---

[19] "Why Intake of Women into Medical Faculty Cut: Toh," *The Straits Times*, March 17, 1979, 13; Quoted in Margaret Thomas, "Goodbye to Those Days, When Women Were 'Pieces of Meat for Men to Slice'," *CNA*, March 31, 2021, https://www.channelnewsasia.com/news/commentary/womens-rights-singapore-issues-history-parliament-gender-equalit-13230626.

policy resulted in "less qualified" male students being admitted to National University of Singapore (NUS) Medicine over "more qualified" female students. Many of the female students went overseas to study medicine and never returned to Singapore.[20]

Policies from this era had long-term consequences. For example, a 2020 article in the Singapore Medical Association's newsletter said that the one-third quota was a major reason that the National Healthcare Group has only 27 per cent women in its senior leadership posts.[21]

Policy 2: Medical Benefits for Families of Civil Servants

In the 1980s, the government passed a policy that extended medical benefits to the families of male civil servants. The same treatment was not given to female civil servants. The reason being that it cost too much. In 1993, Finance Minister Richard Hu reaffirmed this policy on a different basis. He said:

> *The policy preserves the social structure by supporting the principle of husband-as-head-of-household. It is the husband's responsibility to look after the family's needs, including their medical needs. This is how our society is structured. It would be unwise to tamper with this structure.*[22]

Times have changed much. Ministers would not be able to get away with such sexist statements today.

Medical school quotas and civil servants' medical benefits are just some of the discriminatory policies that were made by the PAP government in the Men's Years. There were others. How does one reconcile these discriminatory policies and the zero presence of female MPs with the PAP's

---

[20] Yunn Hwen Gan and Sophia Archuleta, "Holding Up Half the Sky — Women in Singapore Medicine," *Singapore Medical Association* 52, no. 2 (February 2020): 22.

[21] Ibid.

[22] AWARE, "Remaking Singapore: Views of Half the Nation," 2002, https://www.aware.org.sg/wp-content/uploads/Remaking_Singapore.pdf.

Manifesto, *The Tasks Ahead*, to work for a society where "all people will have equal rights and opportunities, irrespective of sex, race or religion"?

One view is that the PAP government started off with aspirations of gender equality but abandoned them along the way, when the women left the Party. Another view is this: that the government's support for women's empowerment was motivated by economic and political imperatives, not by any intrinsic belief in gender equality.

The PAP's economic strategies were indeed favourable to women but should not be mistaken for a principled commitment to gender equality. Whichever way you see it, it is clear that Men in White were men of their times. They wanted to develop women and men to be economically productive, but where gender was concerned, their ideal of women as the "good housewife", whose job was to care for the family and support their husband's career, served as their paradigm.

This second perspective is supported by some later statements of Prime Minister Lee Kuan Yew, including this one in 1994 where Mr Lee said that "attractive and intelligent young ladies" should go to finishing colleges so that they will be "marvellous helpers of their husband's career."[23]

One might argue that the government itself did not have patriarchal values, but it was just not confident that it could shift patriarchal norms that existed in society. However, we should remember that social engineering is something that the Singapore government is comfortable to do and is good at. As Mr Lee Kuan Yew said in 1987:

> *I am often accused of interfering in the private lives of citizens. Yes, if I did not, had I not done that, we wouldn't be here today. And I say without the slightest remorse, that we wouldn't be here, we would not have made economic progress, if we had not intervened on very personal matters — who your neighbour is, how you live,*

---

[23] Anna Teo, "It's Been an Honour, Mr Lee," *Business Times*, March 24, 2015, https://www.businesstimes.com.sg/government-economy/lee-kuan-yew-dies/its-been-an-honour-mr-lee.

the noise you make, how you spit, or what language you use. We
decide what is right. Never mind what the people think.[24]

Looking back, I think that the government would have been able to work towards changing the patriarchal mindsets of its people. Governments that are less paternalistic than the Singapore government, such as Sweden, have done so.

We will now move on to the next phase of Herstory, which covers the period from 1984 to 2010. This period sees the return of women politicians and activists. I call this third period the "Women Return Period".

The Women Return Period (1984–2010)

Within politics, the PAP recruits four women politicians: Dr Dixie Tan, Dr Aline Wong and Mrs Yu-Foo Yee Shoon are elected in 1984 (after a 14-year lull), and Dr Seet Ai Mee is elected in 1988. These women set up the PAP Women's Wing in 1989. Dr Wong and Mrs Yu-Foo are particularly active in pushing for women's rights, but the female politicians are a small minority and none of them are ever given a Cabinet appointment.

On the civil society side, things start to get active again. In 1980, leaders from various women's business and community groups come together to form the Singapore Council of Women's Organisations (SCWO). The SCWO is set up as an umbrella body of women's groups to advance the status of women.

In 1984, the government launches its highly controversial programme, the Graduate Mothers' Scheme, to incentivise graduate mothers to have more children. At the same time, the government introduces the Small Family Incentive Scheme to disincentivise non-graduate mothers from having more than two children. These eugenic programmes upset many women and lead to the formation of the Association of Women for Action and Research (AWARE) as a women's rights research and advocacy group.

---

[24] Quoted in "Government's Hard-Nosed Approach Defended," *The Straits Times*, April 20, 1987, 15.

With women activists back in the picture, the campaign for women's rights is reignited. This time, the burning issue is family violence. AWARE's Women's Helpline shows that family violence is prevalent. Yet, the laws are inadequate. When the police are called in, they can only stop the fight if it is still going on. But unless there are broken bones, an eye, ear or limb hanging out (what the law calls "grievous hurt"), the police have no powers to proceed with an investigation.

AWARE, the Singapore Association of Women Lawyers and the SCWO work together to campaign for more protection against family violence. Dr Kanwaljit Soin, the moderator of this lecture and probably the most well-known women's rights champion of our time, is appointed as a Nominated Member of Parliament (NMP). Dr Soin reaches out to a few other lawyers and me one day, and says, "I would like to introduce a Family Violence Bill. Will you help me to draft this? Malaysia has just passed a Family Violence Bill."

I am game and we are off. These are the pre-Internet days, so it is not so easy to find precedents. The Family Violence Bill is introduced in Parliament in 1995. This is the second Private Members' Bill to be presented in Parliament ever.

One of the main challenges to the Bill is the argument that stronger laws may hurt rather than help families. But the ground support for this Bill is strong thanks to public education, talks and exhibitions that women's rights non-governmental organisations (NGOs) have organised over the previous decade. I remember the second reading well. Dr Soin steps up to the podium and gives a brave and stirring speech. There is a robust debate on the Bill.

The result: Parliament rejects the Family Violence Bill. The government says that the issue is not so prevalent that we need a separate Act to deal with it. Nevertheless, it is a victory for women as the government comes up with an alternative proposal to amend the Women's Charter to strengthen its Personal Protection Order (PPO) regime.

The amended Women's Charter (1996) contains many of the provisions that were in the Family Violence Bill. For example, it expands the definition of family violence to include non-physical violence, and extends protection to a wider range of family members. Most importantly, the Bill empowers the police to act upon the breach of a PPO without there being grievous hurt.

The government goes much further than just amending the law. It sets up a network of Family Service Centres (FSCs) and specialist centres to support family violence survivors. It links these centres to the police, hospitals and the Family Court. This National Family Violence Networking System (NFVNS) has been an important part of Singapore's ongoing strategy to address family violence.

The Lesson

What is the lesson here? We see an old pattern:

1) Women's rights groups raise early warning signals about a social problem;
2) the issue gains traction with the public;
3) within the political system, women activists (in this case, Dr Soin as NMP) push for legal change; and
4) change happens after about 10 years of sustained advocacy.

This pattern of change is not ideal to move the needle on gender equality. It is unreliable, being dependent on the presence and sustained work of a few brave women's activists or NGOs to raise individual issues. Progress comes in spurts, followed by long intervals of non-activity and periods of backsliding.

A strong women's movement is necessary but not sufficient to ensure progress. What we need for more consistent progress is an explicit commitment by the government to gender equality. A commitment with accountability. Do we have this today? Many of you, if you have been following the story so far, might think not. But something rather unexpected happens in 1995.

Seemingly out of the blue, the government ratifies the UN Convention to End All Forms of Discrimination against Women (CEDAW). The pressure to sign did not come from the women activists in Singapore. It came from outside Singapore. Singapore signed CEDAW to be a good global citizen. At least two-thirds of the countries in the world had signed at least one UN Human Rights treaty. Singapore had signed none. As Singapore's presence on the world stage was growing, it is likely that the nation state sought to "fit in" and show its support for the UN Human Rights system.

Of all the human rights conventions, the treaties on Women and Children were the easiest for Singapore to adopt. Singapore was already compliant with many of the provisions in these two treaties. It was more difficult for Singapore to sign treaties on civil and political rights.

The government's ratification of CEDAW is significant. By signing, Singapore committed to protecting and promoting women's rights and to addressing negative gender norms and stereotypes. Every five years, the government reports to the UN CEDAW Committee on what it has done to reduce gender discrimination in Singapore. Singapore has gone through five cycles of reporting to the UN. It has made good progress with each cycle. For example, by the second round of reporting in 2007, the state had reversed all the sexist policies that it enacted during the "Men's Years".

Singapore NGOs are encouraged to and do participate in the CEDAW process by submitting reports to the UN on Singapore's compliance with CEDAW. The UN Committee, after hearing the government's and NGOs' submissions, issues recommendations to the government advising them on further steps it should take to reduce discrimination against women. CEDAW has provided the government and NGOs with a fantastic process for ensuring that Singapore makes consistent progress towards eliminating gender discrimination. The CEDAW process has contributed to many positive changes in policy, including the introduction of the Protection from Harassment Act, Prevention of Human Trafficking Act and removal of marital rape immunity.

However, this does not mean that gender equality has become a fundamental value of Singapore society. When we think of values associated with Singapore, words like meritocracy, multiculturalism and pragmatism pop up in our heads. Few people would associate gender equality with Singapore, the way they do with Nordic countries. Because even though the government signed CEDAW, it has not really been very active in tackling the sexist norms that lie at the heart of the gender equality flower. However, the next phase of Herstory, which I call "Ground-Up Activism", sets the context for the government to initiate the gender equality review.

Ground-Up Activism (2011–Present)

Social media has changed the way we live, including the way that people carry out activism and social justice. There is no specific event to mark the start of this current phase, where ground-up activism is enabled and powered by Facebook, Instagram, YouTube and Twitter. The year that I have chosen as the start year, 2011, is somewhat arbitrary and subjective. It is the year of "SlutWalk Singapore".

SlutWalk Singapore — the name itself seemed almost too provocative and bold for Singapore during that time. I am not sure how many of you have heard of it or remember it. The name stuck in my mind, as did the cause to organise a march in Singapore to end slut shaming and victim blaming of sexual assault survivors. The Singapore march was part of a global response to a Canadian policeman's remark that "Women should avoid dressing like sluts in order to not be victimised." Fifty other slutwalk marches were being held across the globe. It was remarkable. One comment by a Canadian policeman whose name no one remembers inspired 50 protest marches in the world, including a Singapore protest in Hong Lim Park.

Of course, I was impressed by the confidence and gung-ho spirit of the very young activists — they were in their early 20s. But what was more amazing to me was how these activists with no prior experience could, in record time, relying mainly on social media posts going viral, organise a globally-inspired event, which ended up being covered in the *Wall Street Journal* (WSJ). The article was titled "SlutWalk Singapore Puts Feminism in Focus".[25] I do not even think that any of AWARE's campaigns, with 35 years of activism under its belt, has been the feature of a *WSJ* article.

This to me signified the start of the exciting new era of social justice activism. Many of these campaigns — because they are responding to a particular moment in time — do not last long. SlutWalk Singapore lasted two years and disappeared after that. But they certainly are effective in provoking new conversations and ideas, engaging the community and are often precursors to future initiatives that may have more lasting impact.

Social media, high education levels and increased exposure of younger Singaporeans to global conversations have resulted in gender equality and feminism becoming widely discussed topics in Singapore. Established groups like AWARE, Humanitarian Organization for Migration Economics (HOME) and United Women Singapore have also become very adept at using social media to generate public support for their causes. For example, in the last few years, AWARE has effectively used comics, videos, podcasts, online theatre and online petitions to garner support for its causes.

Groups like Beyond the Hijab build purely online communities to create awareness of Muslim women's issues through stories. Many young activists learnt about feminism through Instagram. They engage actively with feminist posts on a daily basis, on topics ranging from rape myths and sexual consent to workplace discrimination and migrant spouses. Last year alone, AWARE's posts across all its social media platforms had a reach of more than 10.6 million.

Global movements like #MeToo have had a sharp and long-lasting impact on sexual assault and harassment in Singapore. AWARE's Sexual Assault Care Centre (SACC) experienced a 79 per cent increase in calls right after #MeToo started. The number of calls to SACC remain at that high-water mark.

We have also seen the private sector, especially the multinational corporations (MNCs) in Singapore, embrace gender diversity in a big way.

---

[25] Chun Han Wong, "SlutWalk Singapore Puts Feminism in Focus," *Wall Street Journal*, December 7, 2011, https://www.wsj.com/articles/BL-SEAB-300.

They do this because gender diversity improves recruitment and the bottom line. And it makes the company look good. Companies set up women's groups and empower them to lead the company's gender diversity agenda in their organisations. These are publicised on the company's website and social media pages. Most larger companies have jumped on the bandwagon to celebrate International Women's Day.

In short, in the last 10 years or so, we have seen a democratisation of the feminist agenda. These are no longer topics that fall within the exclusive domain of feminist activists and experts. Sexism, misogyny, sexual violence, intersectionality, unconscious bias, gender quotas, power imbalances, motherhood penalty and gender pay gap have become mainstream topics for social justice activists, corporate warriors and ordinary people. These are now seen as everyday problems that people encounter in their workplaces, homes, schools and communities. These are also things that we can talk about openly. Social media has also given us the language to parse and discuss these topics.

Norms have shifted. What used to be commonplace boorish behaviour is no longer tolerated, and offenders can expect to be called out on this. We are all expected to play a part in ensuring environments that are respectful, inclusive and safe. It is against this backdrop that the government launched the gender equality review late last year.

The Time Has Come

On 20 September 2020, Mr K Shanmugam, Minister for Home Affairs and Minister for Law, announced that the government would undertake a comprehensive review of issues affecting women to make gender equality a fundamental value in Singapore society. The original motivation for this review was to tackle gender norms that give rise to sexual offences. In the words of Mr Shanmugam, the objective is to cause gender equality to be "imprinted deeply into our collective consciousness ... . Every boy and girl must grow up imbibing the value of gender equality. They need to be taught from a very early age that boys and girls are to be treated equally and, very importantly, with respect."[26]

Women's rights and gender equality activists are cheering on this progressive initiative. For us working in this area, we were actually taken by surprise. How come? Why now? However, upon deeper reflection of how far society has come in the last 10 years, perhaps we should not be so surprised.

The time has come for gender equality in Singapore.

Society wants this. And the government has responded by initiating the gender equality review. Thus, it is not surprising that the response to the many Women's Conversations that the government has organised has been excellent. Women want more, they want to go deeper. Many men are supportive too, as they know that this will make it easier for them to be more active fathers. There is much to gain from this government-led initiative.

As Minister Shanmugam rightly pointed out, gender equality will reduce sexual assault by addressing the root cause of sexual offences. It will alleviate the caregiving burden that holds women back in the workplace. Gender equality is also good for business and the economy, and gives people equal opportunity to fulfil their potential, regardless of gender. Changing mindsets and implementing more gender equality practices has to be a whole-of-nation project, and a long-term one. But it certainly cannot be achieved without the government taking the lead to set up the infrastructure for this to happen.

Just as women's education and empowerment were essential for our success in the last half century, gender equality will be absolutely critical in the next 50 years to deal with the critical issues of our day — low fertility rates, ageing population, economic inequality and the sexualised world that we live in. I will talk more about this in my next two lectures. I will end my

---

[26] Zhaki Abdullah, "Singapore to Embark on a Review of Women's Issues in Move Towards Greater Gender Equality, Leading to White Paper Next Year," *CNA*, September 20, 2020, https://www.channelnewsasia.com/news/singapore/gender-equality-womens-issues-singapore-to-embark-engagements--13126778.

first lecture with three broad points for the gender equality review, drawing from the lessons of Singapore's Herstory.

First Point: The Gender Equality White Paper

The gender equality review will culminate in a White Paper that sets out a roadmap for making gender equality a fundamental value for Singapore. Many people have expressed hope that the White Paper will not just be fluffy words that express nice sentiments. They want to see substance and commitment. I personally would like to see a White Paper that is bold, visionary, substantive and long-term. It should set out a clear and comprehensive plan on the steps that the government will take to role model, signal and set in place laws, policies and programmes to achieve its objectives.

The White Paper should also encourage and spell out what community, companies and families can do to promote gender equality in Singapore. Like the CEDAW mechanism, which has worked well to advance gender equality, it is important to build in reviews and measures to ensure that we are on track.

Second Point: Working Closely With NGOs and Men

In the past, women's rights and gender equality NGOs have been the driving force of gender equality in Singapore. They are very important stakeholders for the government to engage as they have deep knowledge and experience about the gender issues that their communities face. They also have extensive reach to the people who strongly champion gender equality, as well as those who are affected by sexism and misogyny.

It is important for the government to reach out directly to both individuals and NGOs — both bigger NGOs, like the Singapore Muslim Women's Association (PPIS), AWARE and SCWO, and smaller groups who deal with niche issues like LGBT rights, Muslim rights and sexual violence.[27]

---

[27] Founded in 1952, Persatuan Pemudi Islam Singapura (PPIS) or the Singapore Muslim Women's Association is a non-profit organisation focused on community services in Singapore.

This will deepen the state's understanding of the issues on the ground. And very importantly, men should be involved in this project not just as male allies, but in their own right, as the other side of gender equality. It is important to convene conversations just for men, to allow them to share their perspectives in a safe space.

Third Point: The Constitution and Pledge

Even though the PAP's 1959 manifesto *The Tasks Ahead* referred to equality regardless of "sex", this was not included in the Constitution or the Pledge. We now have a chance to change this.

One of the most visible and substantive actions that the government can take to make gender equality a fundamental value is to add gender equality into the Singapore Constitution and our Pledge. Currently, gender equality does not appear in either of these documents, unlike equality on the basis of race and religion. If gender equality is to be established as a fundamental value in our society, this should be reflected in both the Pledge and the Constitution, which are the two most authoritative expressions of Singapore's values. Imagine, if every day, girls and boys recited:

> *We, the citizens of Singapore, pledge ourselves as one united people, regardless of race, language, religion or gender.*

Gender equality would quickly be imprinted in the collective consciousness of all these young minds. For the Constitution, there are two ways of doing this:

1) Amend Article 12(2) of the Constitution by adding "gender" as a prohibited basis for discrimination.
2) To add a new clause that is aspirational.

In my view, the first option is preferable, as that would be better aligned with the state's intention to make gender equality a fundamental value of our society. Such an amendment will ensure that the government and our laws do not discriminate on the basis of gender.

The UN CEDAW Committee has regularly recommended that Singapore include protections against gender discrimination in its Constitution. Of all Constitutions in the world, 85 per cent have explicit prohibitions against gender discrimination. All new Constitutions enacted since 2000 have included this protection.[28]

If it is not feasible to amend Article 12(2), there should, at the very least, be an aspirational provision on gender equality to signify Singapore's commitment to gender equality. Even if it is not binding on the state, an aspirational section carries a strong symbolic value. Symbols are important when we are trying to shift mindsets.

Conclusion

This brings me to the end of this first lecture. What a journey — from the 1950s to where we are today. I hope that you enjoyed the lecture and leave feeling informed about the past, and hopeful about the future. Women in Singapore are highly educated and empowered, but we don't have equality yet.

The substantive issues that I will deal with, to further this conversation, are:

a) Support for Caregiving and Equality at Home, which is my next lecture;

b) Women's Leadership, Men and Masculinity, and Male Violence Against Women, which will be covered in my final lecture.

The road to equality is long and arduous, but we are moving in the right direction. I feel confident about the gender equality review. The ground is so ripe for this, and the government is doing the right thing, at the right time.

---

[28] World Policy Analysis Center, "Constitutional Equal Rights Across Gender and Sex," January 2020, https://www.worldpolicycenter.org/sites/default/files/Fact%20Sheet%203%20-%20Constitutional%20Equal%20Rights%20Across%20Gender%20and%20Sex.pdf.

Question-and-Answer Session
Moderated by Dr Kanwaljit Soin

Dr Kanwaljit Soin: It is a great pleasure for me to be here today, and I am very glad that so many of you have tuned in. I look forward to your participation. As Corinna has mentioned, she and I go a long way back. I have known her for 30 odd years and she has become a great leader for both women and men. She advocates passionately for gender equality, but in a way that inspires others to join her. Kudos to that.

She is the feminist daughter that I never had — but I have three feminist sons. Since I am talking about feminism, I would like to clarify what feminism means to me. A feminist is someone who accords equal respect and consideration to all sexes and genders. And so, I am sure that many of you in this audience also consider yourselves feminists. We have heard an excellent and insightful lecture from Corinna. She has delivered the first instalment of a three-part magnum opus and I salute her for her content, clarity and delivery.

Before the virtual floor is open to everyone in the audience, I would like to ask Corinna the first question. How do you think the government and women's organisations can work together to advance gender equality in Singapore?

Ms Corinna Lim: I think there are several phases to the whole gender equality review. The first phase is the consultation. It would be great if there were opportunities not only for the women's rights and gender equality groups but also for men's groups to be able to provide in-depth feedback to the government.

A lot of the conversations now are more focused on individuals, which I think is really fantastic. What I love about this initiative is that it is a people's movement. And as I have said, gender equality has become a people's issue in the last 10 years, so it is great that the government is so actively consulting with the ground.

Gender advocacy groups have been working in this area for many years. We hear thousands of stories and have been thinking for a long time about what the solutions should be. So, there should be opportunities to have that in-depth discussion.

I am wondering whether it might be possible for the government to set up a multi-group committee, where different organisations will be represented. Take the gender equality flower and divide it up into subgroups, so that there will be working groups going forward. Accordingly, it becomes the work and the accountability of not just the government but the stakeholders in this area that already have such a big interest in this, who will work with the government to take it forward.

I also see a lot of companies that set up a women's group, but when these groups ask for some funding to do something, there is none. So, I think there needs to be resources that actually go to realise this.

It is a very ambitious idea to make gender equality a fundamental value and collective consciousness imbibed by everybody. It needs to be long term and requires resources so individuals and groups can tap on this to further the cause.

AWARE has quite a few programmes. Birds & Bees for parents and Sexual Assault First Responder Training are two examples. We would like to upscale these programmes but we are unable to due to insufficient staffing. But if there were more resources, certainly we can do more of these Sexual Assault First Responder Trainings, for which we have a waitlist of 200 people. So, there are all these existing, ongoing programmes, which I think would be great to work with the government on.

Dr Soin: Thank you. The audience has been waiting so patiently and we will turn to their input and questions. The first two questions are on societal norms. Do you think that the lack of female representation in government during the 1970s and 1980s was caused more by societal norms, rather than by the government? Where do you think these societal norms come from and why do they continue to persist?

Ms Lim: It is hard to draw a line between the two. Like I said, the government were men of their times. The society and ordinary people were not so much into gender equality. During those days I suppose, aside from the Singapore Council of Women's goal to outlaw polygamy, there were not all these conversations, and there were no women's rights groups. So, I do not think gender equality was a big deal in society then. Whoever gets into government has the responsibility to recruit and to look for specific talent.

Today's government is looking for women and want to recruit more women. It is hard to get more women. In those days, I do not think this was their priority, because they did not have those values of trying to achieve equal representation or some representation.

Dr Soin: If I may add to that, the PAP was the only effective party at that time. There was not much political competition. And as you said quite rightly, it was the PAP that went out to look for political candidates, and being men of their time, they missed out on the women. So, it was not just societal norms, I think, that held women back. It was the lack of search for women too.

Ms Lim: This is why I mentioned Chan Choy Siong's background. She was not highly educated, and Ho Puay Choo was, in fact, a seamstress who could not speak English. So, it wasn't so much then that you needed to have very high academic credentials. If you went out to look, you could find other women, like Chan Choy Siong and Ho Puay Choo, who were passionate about nation-building to be in the Party.

Dr Soin: There is a historical question and this is going to be a little bit harder, I think. Did other political parties in the 1950s and 1960s also have manifestos for women to have equal rights? If so, what are the details, and what did they fight for?

Ms Lim: As far as I know, other political parties did have women's rights included in their manifestos. However, they gave less emphasis to this than the PAP and had fewer women candidates. These parties did say we should have women's rights, but they did not do anything about it. You can see this in some of the debates on the Women's Charter, because some of these parties did actually speak up but the PAP would say, "What did you do for women's rights?" So, the PAP certainly was way more progressive than any other parties in this regard.

Dr Soin: From my reading of it, I think the activists did go to the other parties, but they said the time was not right yet to include women's issues in the manifesto.

Now there is a question on the gender equality review. What would make AWARE think that the gender equality review is a success?

Ms Lim: That is a good question. So, you have the gender equality petals, and you will want some movement in each of these petals and try to change gender norms as well. Norms are harder to measure but a good one is the World Values Survey, which has been recently carried out by IPS in 2021. Also, I think a really good measurement would be if there are more stay-at-home dads. During my research, I spoke to three — it was not so easy to find them — and it has not been easy for them as dads. They love spending time with their kids and my heart goes out to them, because I feel I should be fighting for their rights and, in doing this, we are.

So, I think that is a really good measurement because once the dads feel that they can be the primary caregiver, then women can do more in the workplace and have more choices.

Dr Soin: Besides the biological act of giving birth, the ability to look after a child is not controlled by genes. It just so happens that societal norms dictate women's caregiving as the natural order of our culture.

Ms Lim: This is one of the biggest norms that is hard to tackle right now, but it is already changing a little. The ultimate goal is coming to a stage where both parties are seen as caregivers, as well as breadwinners. We need to ensure that the person who is the caregiver is not disadvantaged and is respected, regardless of gender.

Dr Soin: Now another interesting question. What are the barriers to inserting a gender equality clause in Article 12(2) of the Constitution?

Ms Lim: Like I said, Article 12(2) is not an anti-discrimination act. It really is a clause that will be binding on the government. It means that the government cannot have any laws that are not gender equal. So, you can think of some policies and laws already. The Women's Charter's provision on maintenance — it is not equal. Only men with disabilities are entitled to get maintenance from their wives. CareShield is also not equal — women's groups have been fighting and pushing back against the higher premiums. So, the government would have to review those.

It does not have to happen tomorrow. You can say, we want to try to move towards a gender neutral and gender equal state where all laws and policies are not in any way differentiated by gender. That needs to happen, so that in the future we are protected against any discriminatory or differential laws.

Dr Soin: The next one has to do with social media activism. And the question is, the rise in social media activism for gender empowerment has helped to raise awareness among many young Singaporeans. Do you think such online conversations can help to facilitate greater offline changes as well?

Ms Lim: Absolutely. In fact, you know we always say for our activism, we meet the people where they are. And the most progressive people in the era of gender equality, and any social activism, are online. So how can we reach out to them, in order to spread the message to the people who are not online?

If we are looking long term at the younger generation, then maybe we don't target the people who are older and are not going to be so interested in this. We target the young parents and adults who are going to be more interested. Also, I think institutions like schools and companies are important places to make sure that they set the environment promoting gender equality.

Dr Soin: Yeah, but don't forget the older people — the mother-in-law, the mother, the grandmother. They are very important too, and we could target them through movies, television, so please do not forget the people of my generation.

Ms Lim: I am thinking that the young people will find ways to actually talk to their parents and the older generation to bring them around. These are all conversations that we can have among the people that you have some influence over. And you can start with very simple things, just like equal chores for boys and girls, where we roster based on age but not sex.

Dr Soin: Now, another good question in the area of law. Is there any chance that we will get an Equal Pay for Equal Work law in Singapore?

Ms Lim: I think that is a very high-hanging fruit. An anti-discrimination law might be a lower-hanging fruit, and we certainly need one because this is a life problem. AWARE runs a workplace harassment and discrimination advisory and we had 200 cases last year. About a quarter of these had to do with maternity discrimination, even though we already have existing maternity protection laws. Ageism is also going to be another big problem, so we need a general anti-discrimination law.

The other thing about gender pay is that it is harder and slightly more difficult to try to measure. So, a gender pay law, for me, should be a secondary goal.

Dr Soin: Casting our minds historically, I think the three commitments that the PAP promised to women in 1959 were to abolish polygamy, to give equal pay for equal work and to declare 8 March as a public holiday. So, it looks like we have only achieved one so far.

Ms Lim: On the issue of equal pay, I think this can be mitigated with the Progressive Wage Model (PWM). A lot of the jobs that women do are really lowly paid, and they are not on this progressive wage ladder. So, I think that would be something to fight for. Waitresses, teachers, nurses and some of the other more female-dominated sectors like health assistance and healthcare should be on the wage ladder.

Dr Soin: Yeah, but I suppose what the questioner was referring to is Equal Pay for Equal Work.

Ms Lim: The gender pay gap difference is 6 per cent. The total unadjusted is 16 per cent, but that's because women give up work or they take different jobs.[29] But when you talk about equal work, that difference is 6 per cent. If I have to rank this, I will say, an anti-discrimination law comes first, followed by making sure that the women's jobs, especially the ones that are very lowly paid like childcare and eldercare, are put on the PWM as quickly as possible.

Dr Soin: We will go on to the next question. Could you talk a bit about the evolution of the Women's Charter Act over the years? It is sometimes called a "Women's Bill". Does it live up to its name?

Ms Lim: That is really interesting because one of the big criticisms when it was first introduced in Parliament was that this is a very elevated name. It is a Women's Charter but you are only dealing with polygamy and ensuring women can sign contracts, etc.

---

[29] The unadjusted gender pay gap provides raw figures on the differences in pay between men and women, without consideration of various factors that could influence the pay gap comparison. The adjusted gender pay gap measures the gender pay gap between men and women after adjusting for factors such as age, education, occupation type, industry and number of hours worked.

The criticism was that it does not deal with equal pay nor does it ensure that women have equal opportunities in the workplace. So, I think the Women's Charter is misnamed, and I feel strongly that we ought to change the name from the Women's Charter to the Family Charter.

It is far more accurate — 90 per cent of the provisions are about family law. A lot of men object to gender equality on two grounds: one, National Service (NS); two, that you have laws protecting women but not men. The Women's Charter has that name because historically it abolished polygamy. It doesn't give equal rights in the workplace or anywhere else. So, I don't think it's the right name for that charter.

Dr Soin: And it gives the wrong impression that women get some privileges that men don't get.

Well, I am afraid it is time to end this lively discussion and say a big thank you to all of you for your meaningful input. Apologies for the fact that not all comments and questions were addressed, but hopefully the next two lectures will provide more enlightenment on many of these issues.

Now, allow me to close the session with a few words. Gender equality does not mean giving something to women, by taking something away from men. It is not a zero-sum game. Instead, the two parts add up to more than one whole. That is why we must strive for gender equality. It ensures people-centred sustainable development. We cannot have Singapore operating at half strength. We cannot waste half the brains, half the inspiration, half the beauty and joy, and half the human resources of Singapore. So, let us all work together to advance gender equality in our beloved nation. *Majulah Singapura!*

Lecture II

THE CARING ECONOMY

LECTURE II

We, the citizens of Singapore,
pledge ourselves as one united people,
regardless of race, language, religion or gender
to build a democratic society
based on justice and equality
so as to achieve happiness, prosperity
and progress for our nation.

Good afternoon, everyone. Thank you all for coming to my second lecture. I am really glad that you are here. I am happy to report that from my first lecture, my revised version of the pledge incorporating gender was well received by the media as a way of imprinting gender equality into our collective consciousness.

In this lecture, I go further to talk about our continuing project to build a just and equal society "to achieve happiness, prosperity and progress for our nation". Today, we zoom in on the issues of caregiving, work, fertility, ageing and gender.

In my first lecture, I referred to the six core dimensions of gender equality that are most relevant to Singapore. Today, I will deal with the dimension of "equal distribution of unpaid housework and caregiving".

Why? First, because it is a laggard and much more needs to be done. Second, and more importantly, it is holding back women's progress in other areas, especially in the economy and leadership dimensions (the green and light blue petals).[1] Third, because this might help Singapore reverse its declining fertility rate.

The main norm we have to change is this idea that men should be the primary breadwinner, and women the primary caregiver of the family.

Caregiving for our young and old is central to:

• Our low fertility rates
• Women leaving the workforce prematurely
• Care for our ageing population

These are important issues for Singapore, and I will be dealing with each of them in turn.

Getting men to share the care more equally at home is part of the solution. I believe many men are ready and want to do this. With the right laws, and support from employers, we can make this happen.

Of course, it takes more than gender equality in the family to support a family's caregiving needs. In the first 100 days of his presidency, US President Joe Biden released a massive infrastructural proposal that included family leave, investments in childcare and at-home care for the elderly and disabled, alongside plans to rebuild crumbling roads and bridges. What was inspiring to me was the idea that childcare, eldercare, cooking and cleaning were seen to be just as vital to the functioning of the economy as roads and bridges.

Care work is infrastructure.

What Singapore needs is a robust care infrastructure to support our families' care needs — both childcare and eldercare. Without a strong care

---

[1] Refer to Figure 1 in Lecture 1.

infrastructure, our economy and our society just will not tick. That is why this lecture is titled "The Caring Economy".

First, let me start with a teaser for all of you. "Who cooked Adam Smith's dinner?" I believe many of you would have heard of Adam Smith, also known as the "father of capitalism". In his seminal book, titled *The Wealth of Nations* (1776), Smith used the answer to the question "Who cooked Adam Smith's dinner?" to formulate his thesis of capitalism. Adam Smith's dinner comprised bread, beer and steak. So, his answer to the question was the baker, the brewer and the butcher. Why did they do it? Because of their own self-interest, which gave rise to what Smith called the "invisible hand" that drives capitalist markets.

However, Adam Smith overlooked someone important — his mother, Margaret Douglas. Adam Smith lived most of his life with Margaret, who cared for him and their home. Margaret cooked and served the steak. But she is completely left out of the picture, together with the wives of the baker, the brewer and the butcher.

Unfortunately, this incomplete picture of how a capitalist society operates has become the paradigm of economic life. Family care work that is generally carried out by women does not get counted. And so, it does not count. It does not count in the gross domestic product (GDP) and continues to be overlooked and undervalued by policymakers.[2] Yet, capitalism depends upon this very work. Without people caring for the workers, the economy would collapse!

We saw this quite clearly when schools and childcare centres closed during the lockdown. Care and work collided under one roof — people's homes. Without childcare, parents were struggling to get anything else done with their kids at home. Many men also realised for the first time how much caregiving and housework their wives were doing, on top of their paid work. We read reports and heard stories that men stepped up to help. I do not know whether this has continued post-lockdown.

The point is: If we do not see the caregiving being done, because we are outside working or it is taken care of by someone else, we may not realise

---

[2] Katrine Marçal, *Who Cooked Adam Smith's Dinner? A Story About Women and Economics* (London: Portobello Books, 2015).

how much work caregiving takes. The undervaluing of family care is very much at the heart of this lecture.

Let me move to the topic of Singapore's abysmally low fertility rate.

Low Fertility Rate

Singapore's total fertility rate (TFR) is at an all-time low — 1.10 children per woman.[3] The replacement rate is 2.1. Most developed countries have gone below 2.1, but not as low as us.[4] Lower fertility rates are not necessarily all bad. It is partly a sign of how women and men are finding fulfilment in other areas, beyond raising a family. However, our TFR at 1.10 is considered to be dangerously low.

According to Figure 1, which our then-Deputy Prime Minister Teo Chee Hean presented to Parliament in 2013, the TFR was 1.2, slightly above what it is today.[5] The figure shows that in just two generations, we will have one-third of the Singaporeans we have today. This is why TFR is an existential issue for Singapore.

Figure 1. What does total fertility rate mean?

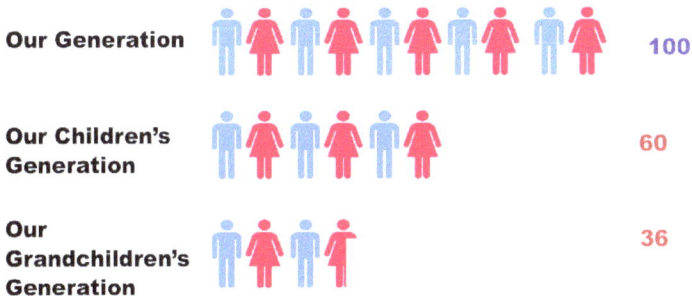

Our Generation	100
Our Children's Generation	60
Our Grandchildren's Generation	36

Source: Adapted from Prime Minister's Office, Strategy Group, "Speech by DPM Teo Chee Hean on Population White Paper at the Parliamentary Debate," February 4, 2013.

---

[3] Hui Min Chew, "Singapore's Total Fertility Rate Falls to Historic Low in 2020," *CNA*, February 25, 2021, https://www.channelnewsasia.com/news/singapore/singapore-total-fertility-rate-tfr-falls-historic-low-2020-baby-14288556.

[4] OECD, "Fertility Rates," accessed April 4, 2021, https://data.oecd.org/pop/fertility-rates.htm.

[5] Adapted from Prime Minister's Office, Strategy Group, "Speech by DPM Teo Chee Hean on Population White Paper at the Parliamentary Debate," February 4, 2013, https://www.strategygroup.gov.sg/media-centre/speeches/speech-by-dpm-teo-chee-hean-on-population-white-paper.

The main concern to address is this: How do we better support the people who want kids?

The government's 2016 Marriage and Parenthood Survey showed that while 92 per cent of married couples would like to have at least two kids, 37 per cent did not achieve their ideal.[6] This was despite the government's efforts to support and promote marriage and parenthood.[7]

Annual spending has increased progressively, by five times, from S$500 million in 2001 to S$2.5 billion in 2017 (Figure 2). Yet the TFR, represented by the pink line, continues to fall. It fell further to 1.10 in 2020.

Why did the pro-natal measures not work? The short answer is that the measures were not sufficient to address the reasons why couples did not want to have kids.[8]

- Too expensive
- Too stressful
- Too difficult to manage work and family demands

These were the reasons given by couples in the same 2016 survey. The issue is not just about money. It is also about time, stress and the actual work of giving care.

The pro-natal incentives were mainly in the form of:

1) Family leave
2) Monetary incentives: baby bonuses, tax breaks and subsidies for pre-school

---

[6] Prime Minister's Office, Strategy Group, National Population and Talent Division, "2016 Marriage and Parenthood Survey," https://www.population.gov.sg/our-population/population-trends/marriage-&-parenthood.

[7] Prime Minister's Office, Strategy Group, National Population and Talent Division, "DPM Teo Chee Hean's Speech on Population at the 2012 Committee of Supply," March 1, 2012, https://www.population.gov.sg/media-centre/speeches/speech-by-dpm-teo-chee-hean-on-population; National Population and Talent Division, "Speech by Senior Minister of State Josephine Teo on Population at the Committee of Supply," March 2, 2017, https://www.population.gov.sg/media-centre/speeches/speech-by-senior-minister-of-state-josephine-teo-on-population.

[8] Prime Minister's Office, Strategy Group, National Population and Talent Division, "2016 Marriage and Parenthood Survey," accessed April 4, 2021, https://www.population.gov.sg/our-population/population-trends/marriage-&-parenthood.

Figure 2.   Singapore's annual budget commitment to Marriage & Parenthood Package versus resident total fertility rate per female

Budget vs Fertility

■ Annual Budget Commitment to Marriage & Parenthood Package
— Resident Total Fertility Rate Per Female

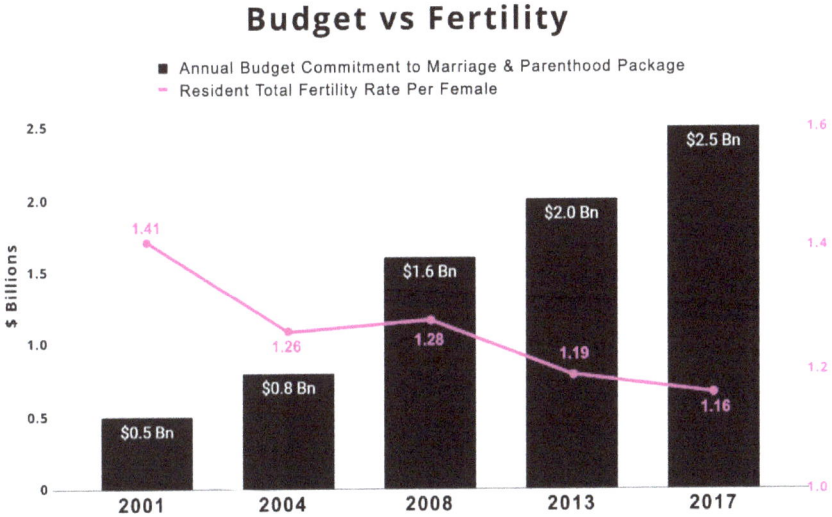

Source: Prime Minister's Office, Strategy Group, "Press Release: Enhanced Marriage & Parenthood Package in Support of a Profamily Environment in Singapore," January 21, 2013; Singapore Department of Statistics, "Resident Total Fertility Rate from 1980 to 2020," June 4, 2021.

Leave is essential, of course, and money is always welcome. But the actual burden of caregiving, especially the burden on mothers, was still not addressed.

Let me move to the related issue of women leaving the workforce prematurely.

Women Leaving the Workforce Prematurely

Girls have overtaken boys in education. Girls do better in school and, on average, have better educational qualifications. But what happens when women and men enter the workforce?

Figure 3.   Resident male and female labour force participation rates across age ranges (2020)

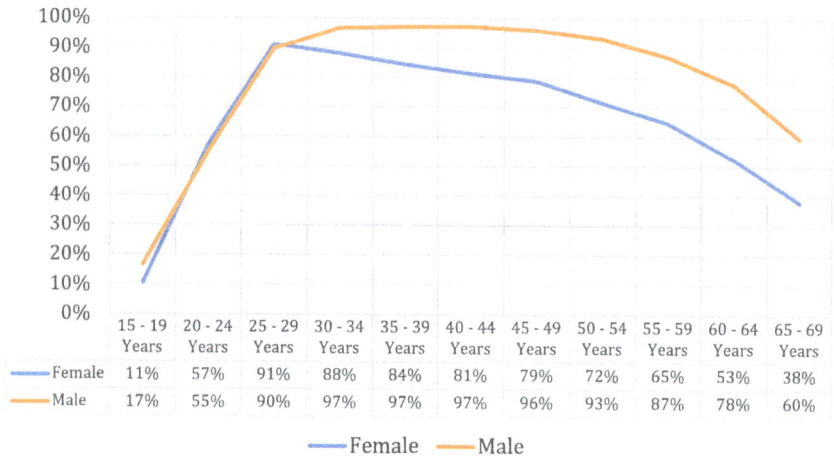

	15 - 19 Years	20 - 24 Years	25 - 29 Years	30 - 34 Years	35 - 39 Years	40 - 44 Years	45 - 49 Years	50 - 54 Years	55 - 59 Years	60 - 64 Years	65 - 69 Years
Female	11%	57%	91%	88%	84%	81%	79%	72%	65%	53%	38%
Male	17%	55%	90%	97%	97%	97%	96%	93%	87%	78%	60%

Female ——— Male

Source: Ministry of Manpower, Manpower Research and Statistics Department, "Labour Force in Singapore: 2020 Edition," January 8, 2021.

Figure 3 shows male and female participation rates in the workforce across age groups — in other words, the percentage of men who are working and the percentage of women who are working. Blue is female. Orange is male.

Let us look at the orange male line first. Between the ages of 25 and 54, close to 100 per cent of men are in the workforce. They start retiring in their mid-50s.

Look at the blue female line. From ages 20 to 29, the two lines run together. The women are no different from the men. The female line peaks at about 90 per cent in the 25 to 29 age group. From ages 30 to 34, it starts to go downhill.

What do you think happens at 30 to 34? If you guessed childbirth, you are absolutely right. The median age of first-time mothers is 30.6 years old.[9] Unlike men, women's ability to work is hampered by child-rearing. This pattern is not too surprising. The same happens in Organisation for

---

[9] National Population and Talent Division, Singapore Department of Statistics, Ministry of Home Affairs, Immigration & Checkpoints Authority, and Ministry of Manpower, "Population in Brief 2020," September 2020, https://www.strategygroup.gov.sg/files/media-centre/publications/population-in-brief-2020.pdf.

Economic Co-operation and Development (OECD) countries. Women stop working when they become mothers. But the difference is that for many OECD countries, including Japan and Korea, women return to the workforce at about 35 to 40 years old, after their children go to school. Their women's curve is in the shape of an "M". The curve goes down, then up, and then down again. For Singapore, the curve just goes downhill all the way.

Why is there no M-curve for Singapore? Why don't our women return to work after their kids start primary school? I have not seen any research on this. But we can make some intelligent guesses:

- Primary School Leaving Examination (PSLE) — women take time off to ensure their kids do well in primary school.[10]
- Ageing parents, as women take time off to look after their ageing parents.
- Ageism, which makes it hard for women and men to return to the workforce at an older age.

How does our labour force participation rate fare against other developed countries?

Figure 4 shows how Singapore's ratio of female to male labour force participation compares to all other OECD countries. Singapore is represented by the red line. The goal is for the ratio to be 100 per cent.

Singapore, the red line, is not vastly behind but we're not ahead either.

At 79 per cent, we are just slightly better than Japan and Korea (the two green lines to the left of the red). And we are behind the best OECD countries, Sweden and Norway, by 10 per cent. Having women drop out of the labour force is a waste of human potential especially given that, on average, Singapore women are more highly educated than men. We must try to do better.

---

[10] For a discussion on the impact this has on mothers, see Teo You Yenn, "'Be Decent Mother, Go Through PSLE': When Children's Education Becomes Parental Care Labor," *Academia SG*, February 24, 2021, https://www.academia.sg/academic-views/be-decent-mother-go-through-psle-when-childrens-education-becomes-parental-care-labor.

Figure 4. Singapore's female-to-male labour force participation rate compared with all OECD countries

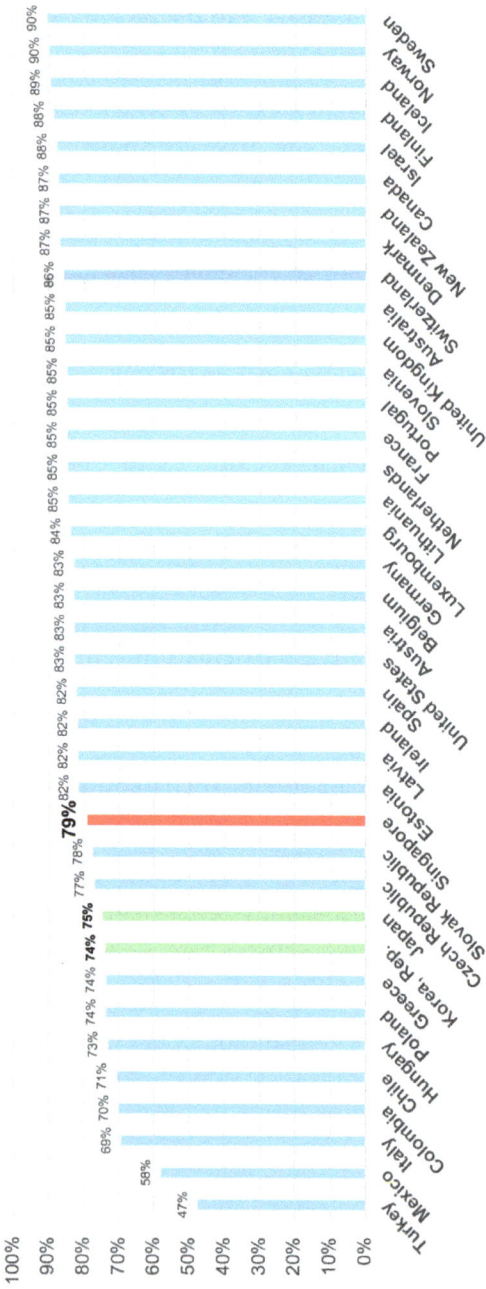

Source: OECD, "Labour Force Statistics by Sex and Age," accessed April 4, 2021, https://stats.oecd.org/Index.aspx?DataSetCode=lfs_sexage_i_r. Ministry of Manpower, Manpower Research and Statistics Department, "Resident Labour Force Participation Rate by Age and Sex," [2020 data], accessed April 4, 2021, https://stats.mom.gov.sg/Pages/LabourForceTimeSeries.aspx.

The issues of women's workforce participation and Singapore's low fertility rates boil down to one thing: the expectation that women, who are now educated and have careers, will continue to bear the brunt of the caregiving burden.

This expectation sets up a situation where women have to choose between their careers and their children. Some give up their careers for family, others choose career over family. Either way, it is not ideal for Singapore. We end up with both low fertility and women leaving the workforce prematurely. Many places, including Korea, Taiwan and Japan, face similar problems.

Can women be supported to pursue their careers and have kids? Countries like Sweden, Norway, Iceland and Finland have shown that it is possible. With the right family support and care policies, a country can have it all — high fertility, working mothers, a competitive economy and also very happy citizens. You know, the Nordics always top the charts for happiness.

The experience of these countries shows that there are two things that governments can do to increase fertility and women's workforce participation rates:

1) Embed gender equality into laws and policies. In particular, use parental leave policies to nudge husbands to be more active fathers. What I call the "gender equality solution".

2) Build a robust care infrastructure to support all families' caregiving needs.

We need to do both. Let's look at the gender equality solution first.

Gender Equality Solution

The Nordic experience has shown that the best way to change societal norms on parenting is to give men and women equal parenting leave. If men do not take their leave, they will lose it. So, many take it, and end up loving it.

As the Swedish Ambassador to Singapore Niclas Kvarnström said during a gender equality discussion, "no one ever regrets it". He has four kids and took "daddy days" for all of them.[11] The norms have changed so much in Sweden that fathers who do not take paternity leave are frowned upon.

Research has shown that dads who are actively involved in the early months of their kids' lives are much more likely to be active fathers in later years. They also share domestic work and paid work more equitably with their partners beyond the paternity leave period.

As part of its pro-natal measures, Singapore extended paternity leave to two weeks in 2017. In 2019, 55 per cent of eligible men took their paternity leave.[12] To me, this is a positive sign of how societal norms are changing quite rapidly.

These days, it is quite common to see dads walking around with their kids strapped onto their chests. Or jogging, cycling, going to the store with their kids in hand. No mothers in sight. More fathers have become active parents although mothers still do the bulk of the work at home.[13]

This pro-natal strategy is definitely worth pursuing because it benefits families directly, and also creates a more gender equal and pro-family culture.

Two weeks of paternity leave was a good start but it is insufficient for fathers who want to be equal parents. How much can a person do in two weeks? That might just be enough time for fathers to get the hang of things. So, we see companies like Aviva, Diageo and HP voluntarily giving four months of paternity leave to their male employees in Singapore. They understand that this is a good way to attract and retain talent.

---

[11] Niclas Kvarnström, personal communication with Corinna Lim, April 16, 2021.

[12] According to the Ministry of Manpower (MOM), eligible working fathers are entitled to two weeks of government-paid paternity leave. Working fathers can also apply to share up to four weeks of their wives' 16 weeks of government-paid maternity leave, under Singapore's shared parental leave policy.

[13] Wei-Jun Jean Yeung and Centre for Family and Population Research, "Singapore Longitudinal Early Development Study Research Update Issue 2," National University of Singapore, July 2020, https://fass.nus.edu.sg/cfpr/wp-content/uploads/sites/17/2020/09/Research-Update_Issue-2_July-2020_opt.pdf.

I also spoke to two parents, Ken and Liz, about their experiences. Ken is the father of a 10-year-old boy. He shared his parenting experience about why men should have longer paternity leave. He said:

> When I became a father I relished being a freelancer because I had flexible hours that allowed me to spend a lot of time with my son and assume my rightful half of childcare duties.
>
> At the same time, I wondered about other fathers — fathers who had full-time jobs but only scant paternity leave. I know that even if I were working as an employee in a company, I'd want to have as much paid leave for childcare as any new mother.
>
> My body, unlike my wife's, did not need physical healing and regeneration for breastfeeding after my son's birth. Therefore, it was all the more important to me that I could do the diaper changing, share in the sleepless nights through bottle feeding and, as my son grew older, spend as much time with him as a stay-at-home dad as possible.

Today, Ken enjoys a wonderful relationship with his son. He tells me:

> In many ways my son is as close to me (if not closer) than to his mum. Sometimes when he's troubled he'll come to me first. He looks to me for comfort and play but also for the conventional "mum" things — preparing food, sending him to soccer classes, story and bedtime routine.

Ken's wish list for policy changes include:

- Paid paternity leave equal to what mothers have.
- Unisex toddler stations or diaper-changing facilities in men's toilets. (He has had to change his son on the top of a wet-wiped toilet seat too many times.)

Liz is the mother of a five-month-old baby. She shared the importance of having the support of her partner:

> *One obstacle I've faced is the unequal amount of parental leave my partner and I have. As he only had two weeks, I gave my partner my shareable month. So, he had a total of one and a half months and I had three months.*
>
> *I had a condition where I felt a burst of negative emotions right before breastfeeding. Having my partner's presence at home was very helpful for me to cope.*
>
> *My partner had to return to work during my maternity leave which meant I had to do things like lifting the baby out of the cot myself, going against my physiotherapist's advice to not exert myself three months post C-section.*

While not everyone is ready to take more than two weeks of paternity leave, our policies should support those who are keen to do so.

The other unsatisfactory issue about the current leave is the disparity between mothers' and fathers' leave. Currently, mothers have four months' maternity leave. Fathers have two weeks' paternity leave. This huge disparity reinforces the idea that child-rearing is primarily the mother's

Figure 5.   Total paid leave per family

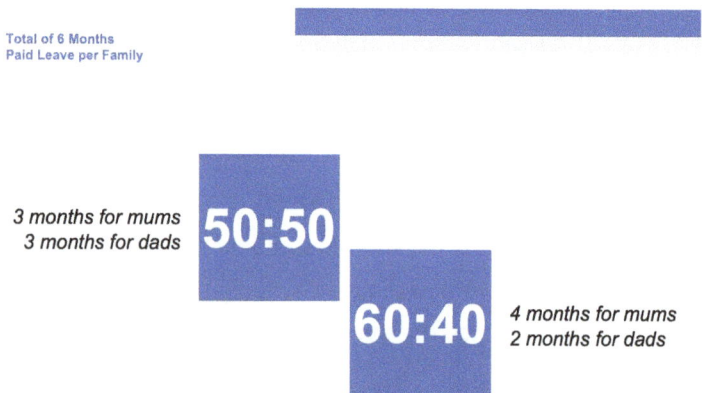

Total of 6 Months
Paid Leave per Family

3 months for mums
3 months for dads
50:50

60:40
4 months for mums
2 months for dads

role. It goes against the idea of gender equality and hurts women's career prospects.

The gender equality review presents us with a wonderful opportunity to update our paternity leave provisions. Ultimately, we should aim for a situation where all parents have the same amount of parenting leave, regardless of gender. If mothers have four months, fathers should have four months too. But this needs long-term consideration and planning, as employers will be greatly impacted by this. In the meantime, here is my recommendation to equalise paternity leave as part of the gender equality review:

Increase the total paid leave for the family to a maximum of six months, where fathers can take two to three months' leave, and mothers can take three to four months' leave. That means parents can decide if they want to split their leave (Figure 5):

a) 50:50 — three months for mothers and three months for fathers; or

b) 60:40 — four months for mothers and two months for fathers

I am a huge advocate of active fatherhood for many reasons. Aside from the ones that I have shared, here are a few more:

First, active fatherhood is great for kids. Research shows that when fathers are more involved, kids do better in school, are more empathetic and have higher self-esteem and life satisfaction.[14] They do not get into as much trouble and are less likely to engage in substance abuse.[15]

Second, it is great for dads too. Fatherhood improves men's health, self-esteem and sense of purpose in life.[16] Dads take their health more seriously and reduce risk-taking behaviours.[17]

---

[14] William H. Jeynes, "A Meta-Analysis: The Relationship Between Father Involvement and Student Academic Achievement," *Urban Education* 50, no. 4 (2015): 414; Annabel Amodia-Bidakowska, Ciara Laverty, and Paul G. Ramchandani, "Father-Child Play: A Systematic Review of its Frequency, Characteristics and Potential Impact on Children's Development," *Developmental Review* 57, no. 100924 (2020): 9; Riley L. Marshall, Colin R. Harbke, and Lisabeth Fisher DiLalla, "The Role of Remembered Parenting on Adult Self-Esteem: A Monozygotic Twin Difference Study," *Behavior Genetics* 51, no. 2 (2021): 130–33.

[15] Rebecca Goldman and National Family and Parenting Institute, *Fathers' Involvement in Their Children's Education: A Review of Research and Practice* (London: National Family and Parenting Institute, 2005).

[16] Edward E. Bartlett, "The Effects of Fatherhood on the Health of Men: A Review of the Literature," *The Journal of Men's Health & Gender* 1, no. 2–3 (2004): 165–67; Letitia E. Kotila and Claire M. Kamp Dush, "Involvement with Children and Low-Income Fathers' Psychological Well-Being," *Fathering* 11, no. 3 (Fall 2013): 321–23.

[17] Nan Marie Astone and H. Elizabeth Peters, "Longitudinal Influences on Men's Lives: Research from the Transition to Fatherhood Project and Beyond," *Fathering* 12, no. 2 (Spring 2014): 168–69.

Third, it role models gender equality for our next generation. Women going out to work changed the way that their children thought about women's roles in society.[18] In the same way, men doing more at home will change the way our children see men's roles in society.

In line with the idea that fathers should be equal parents or sometimes even stay-at-home parents, we should also amend the Women's Charter to equalise men's rights to seek maintenance from their wives. Currently, Section 69 of the Women's Charter only allows husbands to apply for maintenance from their wives if they are incapacitated. Meanwhile, wives have an unfettered right to apply for maintenance from their husbands.

The provision reflects the patriarchal norm that men as primary breadwinners have a duty to maintain their wives. It is time to update this provision and give men the same rights as women to apply for maintenance. Where husbands do apply for maintenance, the Courts will make the final decision on whether it is fair to award this.

As the Nordic experience has shown, equal parenting policies are effective in setting more egalitarian gender norms in the family. In Sweden nowadays, it is common to see "Latte Papas". This is an affectionate term for groups of dads who push their prams, go into a café and have a latte.

I cannot wait for the day when "Kopi Papas" becomes a thing in Singapore.

Care Infrastructure

Let's move onto the second solution, building a robust care infrastructure to ease the burden on women. This refers to the state providing public childcare services. In the late 1970s, when the government realised that

---

[18] White Ribbon Campaign, "Give Love, Get Love. The Involved Fatherhood and Gender Equity Project," January 2014, https://www.whiteribbon.ca/uploads/1/1/3/2/113222347/fatherhood_report.pdf; Adrienne Burgess, "The Costs and Benefits of Active Fatherhood: Evidence and Insights to Inform the Development of Policy and Practice," *Fathers Direct*, 2008, https://www.fatherhood.gov/research-and-resources/costs-and-benefits-active-fatherhood-evidence-and-insights-inform-development; Gary Barker, Juan Manuel Contreras, Brian Heilman, Ajay Singh, and Marcos Nascimento, "Evolving Men: Initial Results from the International Men and Gender Equality Survey (IMAGES)," *International Center for Research on Women* and *Instituto Promundo*, June 2011, https://promundoglobal.org/wp-content/uploads/2014/12/Evolving-Men-Initial-Results-from-IMAGES.pdf.

family caregiving was hindering women's participation in the workforce, it launched the Foreign Maid Scheme to enable families to employ foreign domestic workers. At this point, the state did not invest in building public childcare for families. The private market seized this opportunity by offering a range of services that cost as much as S$2,000 per child at the high end.

To me, this is not the usual Singaporean way of doing things.

Our excellent social infrastructure — education, housing, healthcare and transport — has been the cornerstone of our economic success. The state provided high-quality flats, facilities and services to ensure that the basic needs of all Singaporeans were met. The private market exists but is secondary.

Why did the government not, at first instance, invest in building a strong childcare infrastructure in the same way that it built a strong education system? And why did the government start aggressively building childcare infrastructure only after 2012, less than a decade ago, when it has been desperately trying to increase total fertility rates for more than three decades? Why was there a delay of 20 years to build childcare?

I have been researching and pondering about this over the last few months. In my analysis, there are three reasons for this:

1) Let's get back to the Adam Smith story. Unpaid care work is overlooked and undervalued in our capitalist system. Male decision-makers may not have realised that childcare is essential for women to work. A lack of childcare does not impact men's work as much as women.

2) Patriarchal thinking. Women are expected to do the housework and take care of the family. So, if women cannot handle those duties, then pay another woman, a migrant domestic worker, to do this for low wages. No need to provide public services.

3) Elitist or eugenical ideas. Our early leaders, in particular Prime Minister Lee Kuan Yew, were fixated on the elitist idea that intelligence is an inheritable trait. These elitist ideas led the government to

introduce the Graduate Mothers' Scheme in 1984 to incentivise graduate mothers to have kids. Under this Scheme, children of graduate mothers got priority admission to schools.[19]

On the flip side, low-income and poorly educated couples were discouraged from having kids. They were paid S$10,000 to stop at two kids. The Graduate Mothers' Scheme was so unpopular that it was reversed the next year.

However, this elitist way of thinking did not go away.[20] Since the government was not keen for less educated families to have more kids, there was no need to provide childcare services for them. Better-off families could afford their own domestic workers and to pay for private childcare.

Private solutions may seem very attractive. It saves the government from having to take on the burden of managing or providing these services. However, relying on the market to provide solutions to fulfil basic human needs like childcare is deeply concerning as it increases social inequality.

Certainly, in the Association of Women for Action and Research's (AWARE) 2018 research report "Why Are You Not Working?", the lack of accessible pre-school was one of the reasons why low-income mothers were not working.[21] It is only recently that the government focused its attention on ensuring the provision of accessible quality pre-school, when it set up the Early Childhood Development Agency (ECDA) in 2013.

Since then, the state has made great progress in building pre-school infrastructure, including:

- Improving the quality of pre-school services
- Making pre-school more affordable and accessible
- Creating the KidSTART programme to support the healthy development of kids from low-income families.

---

[19] Chua Mui Hoong and Rachel Chang, "Did Mr Lee Kuan Yew Create a Singapore in His Own Image?" *The Straits Times*, March 24, 2015, https://www.straitstimes.com/singapore/did-mr-lee-kuan-yew-create-a-singapore-in-his-own-image.

[20] Ibid.

[21] AWARE, "'Why Are You Not Working?': Low-Income Mothers Explain Challenges with Work & Care," 2018, https://d2t1lspzrjtif2.cloudfront.net/wp-content/uploads/Advocacy-report-why-are-you-not-working-updated-2-April-2019.pdf.

Families who earn less than S$2,500 a month can now pay as little as S$3 a month for full-day childcare, after subsidies.

In 2017, Prime Minister Lee Hsien Loong announced that the government would double its annual spending on the pre-school sector to S$1.7 billion in 2022 — "a heavy investment, but worthwhile and necessary," said PM Lee. In fact, Singapore has increased its annual spending on pre-school to about five times from 2012. From S$360 million, it went up to S$1.7 billion a decade later.[22]

The latest indications are that government-supported pre-school will be available to meet at least 80 per cent of families' needs by 2025. We had a late start and there is still some catching up to do.

Let me go back to my colleague Liz, who shared about her search for infant care.

Liz's Story

Even as I speak, Liz is desperately searching for infant care for her five-month-old baby. She is anxious and stressed, as she has used up all of her maternity leave. Yet she cannot go back to work until she can get a full-day infant care for her daughter. She's been on the waiting list of 10 nearby pre-school centres. This is the maximum number of waiting lists allowed. Her monthly household income is about S$7,000. Sparkletots is the most affordable centre. After subsidies, it will cost the family S$480, about 7 per cent of their income.

One other centre has a space in September, five months from the time she applied. But they are higher-end and charge S$960 per month. At 13 per cent of the family income, it is beyond the couple's budget. But they may have no choice. Many young couples face the same predicament — availability and cost.

The infant care situation should hopefully get better for parents by 2025. Aside from providing more affordable pre-school places, there are other urgent priorities to work on:[23]

---

[22] Priscilla Goy, "Big Increase in Childcare Places, MOE Kindergartens," *The Straits Times*, August 21, 2017, https://www.straitstimes.com/singapore/big-increase-in-childcare-places-moe-kindergartens.

[23] Lasse Lipponen, Lynn Ang, Sirene Lim, Jaakko Hilppö, Hongda Lin, Antti Rajala, and Lien Foundation, *Vital Voices for Vital Years 2* (Singapore: Lien Foundation, 2019).

We do not have enough childcare teachers as the pay and recognition are not great:[24]

1) Childcare fees are still much higher than primary schools. The lowest rate for full-day care is about S$300 a month, compared with primary school fees at S$15. The fees should not depend on whether the mother is working, which is currently the case. Ironically, full-time mothers have to pay more than working mothers.

2) We also need to enable our pre-schools to cater to kids with special needs. There are a growing number of kids with developmental problems such as autism, behavioural issues and speech delays. Currently, early intervention programmes are outside the pre-schools. This makes it extremely challenging for parents who have to transfer their kids from one place to another in the middle of the workday.

I am glad to see the government's current focus and investment in developing pre-school infrastructure.

I've spent some time analysing how our systemic biases hindered the development of a more robust pre-school infrastructure. This is useful when we consider our eldercare approach. The research shows that the availability of formal childcare has a strong positive impact on parents' decisions to have children.[25] I hope that the increased government intervention will lead to higher fertility rates by lowering the care burden on parents.

Beyond Pre-School

So far, I have been focusing on the caregiving infrastructure for children. The education system is a separate but related system.

It used to be a good public system, but these days parents spend a lot of money on tuition to help their kids do well in PSLE. In 2018, Singapore

---

[24] Ibid.

[25] Erin Hye-Won Kim, "Division of Domestic Labour and Lowest-Low Fertility in South Korea," *Demographic Research* 37, no. 24 (July–December 2017).

households spent S$1.4 billion on tuition.[26] Not all of this is for PSLE. But we know that nothing beats PSLE in terms of parental involvement and tuition. The upshot of this is that:

a) Primary school has now become a public-cum-private system that amplifies inequality. Rich kids get tuition in every subject; poor families scrounge around for free tuition in the subjects they need help in.

b) The PSLE system has created a huge amount of unpleasant care labour for parents. Parents spend a lot of time searching for the best tutors, ferrying kids here and there, coordinating timetables, nagging and scolding children, and getting upset with family members because it is all so stressful.

c) It is now quite normal for one parent, usually the mother, to resign from her job or take one year off to support her kids to get through PSLE. A mother whose child was struggling at Primary 5 told me that she quit her job as she felt that she would not be able to live with herself if her child did poorly and she had not done everything she possibly could to support him. It is heartbreaking to hear these stories. This is not what childhood and parenthood should be about.

The PSLE system is clearly not working. This is one of the reasons why I think that our women's labour force participation curve does not have an M shape. Research from East Asia has also shown a negative correlation between TFR and household spending on education.[27]

There have been calls to abolish PSLE. I strongly support that we abolish or overhaul the system. In assessing the system, I hope that policymakers take into account the impact of PSLE on women, our economy, fertility

---

[26] Kelvin Seah, "Tuition Has Ballooned to a S$1.4b Industry in Singapore — Should We Be Concerned?" *Today*, September 12, 2019, https://www.todayonline.com/commentary/tuition-has-ballooned-s14b-industry-singapore-should-we-be-concerned.

[27] Kim, "Division of Domestic Labour," 747.

rates and social inequality. There must be less costly ways to provide our children with a good education.

Will we be able to successfully reverse our fertility rate if we implement the gender equality solution, take away PSLE and make high-quality pre-school universal?

I wish I could guarantee this. I know these solutions will help many families and that it may make it more feasible for people to have kids.

But we also have new challenges ahead of us. One of them is climate change. Kristian and his partner, Heng Yeng, are recent graduates. They are in their mid-20s and part of the climate justice group, SG Climate Rally. They are waiting for their Build-To-Order (BTO) flat, which should be ready by 2023. They have decided not to have any kids for this reason:

> *My partner and I recognise that this world is rapidly deteriorating,*
> *both socio-politically and ecologically. The science shows us that*
> *we are teetering on the edge of no return, with more diseases,*
> *natural disasters and unpredictable changes on the horizon.*
> *Recognising this reality, the conversation around having a child*
> *becomes quite non-negotiable for us: We cannot knowingly bring*
> *a child into this (literal and metaphorical) burning world.*

Even though it sounds somewhat depressing, it is important to know what some members of the younger generation are thinking and to hear their concerns. Singapore and the world have to really think about how people can thrive without over-burdening our planet, without having to rely on economic models that are dependent on population growth. Perhaps this will be the subject of another IPS-Nathan Lecture.

Let's move on to the topic of our ageing population.

Ageing Population

Let me ask you a question. Assuming good health, if you could choose to live either till 64 or 84, what would you choose? This is a no-brainer, right? Most people would choose to live till 84. And that is one of the remarkable benefits of Singapore's development in the last 60 years. Singaporeans are living longer than most nationalities.

The average life expectancy was 64 in 1957 and it is 84 in 2020. We gained an extra 20 years' lease of life. This means that many of us alive today may live to beyond 90 years old. Our longevity is certainly something to celebrate and can be a huge boost to our economy. Older individuals today are generally healthier and wealthier than those from past generations. And they seek to remain engaged and relevant for years beyond the retirement age.

As you know from my last lecture, my feminist mother, Dr Kanwaljit Soin, is 79 and still practises as an orthopaedic surgeon. My real mother, June Lim, is also 79 and still enjoys working as a housing agent. They both do more strenuous workouts than me. I tell them jokingly that when I grow up, I want to be like them.

Older workers offer valuable experience and talent. They provide perspective, experience and stability. Through their insights, they can serve as mentors and role models to younger counterparts. Studies have found that the productivity of both older and younger workers is higher in companies with mixed-age work teams.[28] Also, an ageing population opens up new markets as older people will have different needs. If managed well, our ageing population may indeed be our only increasing natural resource.

However, when people talk about ageing and our ageing population, it is often with a sense of apprehension and anxiety. The images that we associate in our mind with ageing are those of illness, disability, vulnerability, and the sacrifices and burden of caregiving. When we think about the ageing of our older relatives, we worry about the impact it may have on our lives if they should fall sick or become disabled. For example, we worry about whether we:

- will be able to cope with our own families, our jobs and caregiving at the same time;

---

[28] OECD, "Good for Business: Age Diversity in the Workplace and Productivity," in *Promoting an Age-Inclusive Workforce: Living, Learning and Earning Longer* (Paris: OECD Publishing, 2020), 63–64.

- have to change our living arrangements to accommodate our relatives who may need help with daily activities;
- can afford the care that our loved ones need.

In short, the ageing population offers both opportunities and challenges. Here's the thing: we can only reap the benefits of the gift of longevity if we have a strong care infrastructure to support our ageing population's needs.

In other words, we need to meet the challenges before we can reap the benefits of longevity. But more than that, if we fail to meet the challenges, longevity becomes a liability for our economy and society. The stakes are high.

With children, if we don't have a strong care infrastructure, people just won't have babies. With older persons, most people will feel obliged to care for their parents if their parents need their support. It is not a matter of choice. If our parents are unable to cope on their own and if we have to, we will make other adjustments, like give up work at 50. This then leads to further problems down the road for caregivers and society. No longevity benefits, just liabilities.

With these things in mind, let me talk about the current infrastructure of eldercare. The question is: Does our current infrastructure support the people who need care and the people who give care, to enable us to benefit from longevity? From my perspective, the answer is: not yet.

And I am worried about the current pace and trajectory of the development of our eldercare infrastructure for the reasons set out below.

Our current national strategy is to have people age at home — what we call "ageing in place" — rather than in institutions.

Research shows that in most families, care is given by a family member, usually female, supported by a migrant domestic worker.[29]

Sounds familiar, right? That was our childcare strategy too. Of course, not every family can afford to hire a domestic worker. Neither are all

---

[29] ESCAP, "Long-Term Care of Older Persons in Singapore," June 15, 2016, https://www.unescap.org/sites/default/d8files/Theme-Study-References.pdf.

domestic workers fit to look after specific elderly needs and conditions like dementia and stroke.

Currently, family carers have inadequate public support. For example, there is no mandated eldercare paid leave in Singapore. For childcare, each parent is given six days of paid leave. There are formal services like day care centres and homecare services, which are supposed to support family caregivers. However, families do not use them because they are too expensive.[30]

For instance, based on Lien Foundation's report, *Care Where You Are*, a family of three with a household income of about S$8,000 would have to spend nearly a third of their income on eldercare.[31] Overall, the out-of-pocket expenses that families have to pay are much more than for childcare.

There is a shortage of nursing homes, and respite care is difficult to access.

AWARE's research in this area shows the following trends emerging:

Many family members, usually women, are giving up their jobs to take care of their relatives. These family caregivers, mostly in their 50s, are not just disadvantaged by their loss of income and ongoing expenses during the period that they are full-time caregivers. Having disrupted their careers before building up enough savings, many of them eventually need to return to the workforce in their late 50s. However, they face the issues of loss of confidence, workplace ageism and not having kept up with technological change, which make it extremely difficult for them to return.

Many of the family caregivers and domestic workers we interviewed were also suffering from prolonged stress and fatigue and exhibited signs of caregiver burnout.[32]

---

[30] Elaine L. E. Ho, Shiou-Liang Huang, and Lien Foundation, *Care Where You Are* (Singapore: Straits Times Press, 2018), 183.

[31] Ibid.; Shiou-Liang Wee, Chang Liu, Soon-Noi Goh, Wayne F. Chong, Amudha Aravindhan, and Angelique Chan, "Determinants of Use of Community-Based Long-Term Care Services," *Journal of the American Geriatrics Society (JAGS)* 62, no. 9 (2014): 1802.

[32] AWARE, "Make Care Count: The Impact of Eldercare on the Retirement Adequacy of Female Caregivers," September 2019, https://www.aware.org.sg/wp-content/uploads/Aware_Eldercare-Research-Report-8-10-19.pdf; AWARE and HOME, "Neither Family Nor Employee: The Caregiver Burden of Migrant Domestic Workers in Singapore," November 2020, https://www.aware.org.sg/wp-content/uploads/Neither-Family-Nor-Employee-AWARE-HOME-Report-Nov-2020.pdf.

Once again, we undervalue care, and are not investing enough to build a robust eldercare infrastructure. In the case of eldercare, there are also ageist biases that elders are "over the hill" and, economically, provide poor returns on capital. Some people think: if money is limited, invest in kids and compromise eldercare.

If you did think this, I hope that this lecture has shown why we need to invest in both, for our economy to reap the benefits of our human capital. If we do not do this, our workforce and economy will suffer.

When I say building a care infrastructure, I do not mean that it has to be a Housing and Development Board (HDB) model where the government owns everything. The private sector will have a big role to play, but the government must be involved to oversee, fund and manage, as necessary, to ensure that the services are universally accessible to everyone. So, it could be like our education model or childcare model. If there is not enough money for it, we either find money from other sources or raise taxes. We have been too conservative in our long-term care investments.

Just to illustrate, about eight years ago, Singapore started to build more nursing homes. There were calls from the public to provide single or twin rooms. In the end, the government decided on a dorm-style layout of six to eight beds; it is not the ideal layout for a place where people will spend their final years.

I showed people a photo of dorm-style nursing homes and asked if they would like to spend their last years there or put their parents in such nursing homes. Some people thought it was a hospital. I have not found anyone who would like to spend their last years there if they had a choice.[33] With this as the only other alternative, family caregivers feel they have no choice but to take care of the seniors at home, even when they are not in the best position to do so.

I strongly urge the government to review its approach to long-term care. There is a lot at stake for the economy and our society if we do not

---

[33] AWARE, "Make Care Count: The Impact of Eldercare on the Retirement Adequacy of Female Caregivers," September 2019, https://www.aware.org.sg/wp-content/uploads/Aware_Eldercare-Research-Report-8-10-19.pdf; Desmond Ng, "When Carers are Burnt Out, Who Cares for Them?" *CNA*, May 5, 2019, https://www.channelnewsasia.com/news/cnainsider/when-carers-caregivers-burnout-who-cares-them-ageing-elderly-11504380.

invest enough to support our family caregivers. It takes time to build up affordable services, centre-based care, nursing homes, paid leave and a much wider array of residential options.

So, we should start investing more now, and not scramble to do this 10 or 20 years down the road, as we did with childcare. It may call for more taxes, but people will accept the need for higher taxes if they understand how they and their families can benefit. More funding in this area also offers opportunities for the marketplace to innovate technological solutions and services. Given the large cohorts of seniors, the lack of adequate infrastructure will cause a lot of pain in the community.

What is the level of provision that we want to ensure for everyone? What is our standard for nursing homes, homecare services? What level of privacy and comfort will assure people that their dignity will be respected right up till the end? These are important questions for Singapore to think about. Singapore is on its way to having one of the oldest populations in the world. Let us build eldercare systems that we can be proud of; systems that speak to who we want to be as people — decent, caring, compassionate and respectful of our seniors.

The Caregiving Economy

In this lecture, I have covered issues that are most pertinent today and provided recommendations for policy changes that can be affected as part of the gender equality review or in the near future. If we succeed in building a caring economy, what would our society look like in 2050?

Come with me as we journey into the future.

The year is 2050.

Dads are loving being fathers. They cannot get enough of it. Fathers talk about how they see life differently. They talk about how they want to be the best person they can be, for their kids.

We see a lot more children these days. The fertility rate has turned the corner. Our TFR is now at 1.25.

Work has changed a lot because of the pandemic. Working from home has become the norm. It is easier for parents to balance work and family. That is a good thing as it has become really difficult and expensive to hire domestic workers. Many families decide they can do without a live-in domestic worker.

Also, we now have a great childcare system. Childcare quality has been improving every year. Kids with disabilities attend the same childcare as other kids. Singapore is now among the top five childcare systems in the world.

Our long-term care is now number two in the world. Next to Japan. We can be really proud of that, because we came a long way.

Children are enjoying school more. There are no more PSLE. Primary school is more fun. The kids also learn about equality and respect for one another.

Singapore has become a silver-haired paradise. Silver is in. Silver-haired men and women are everywhere, economically active, contributing in many ways, from the Cabinet to boardrooms, malls, fast-food counters and new community centres.

Also, the government has done a good job in making it easy for seniors to travel everywhere easily and for free. Their project to make Singapore a silver-haired paradise works really well.

I write this from my HDB studio apartment in the Yishun HDB retirement village. Many of my friends have moved here as well. It's great. We look out for one another.

That is what I see of the Singapore of 2050. Do you think this is possible? It is important to be able to dream of the society that we want for ourselves. Let us all work to make that dream come true.

This brings me to the end of my second lecture. It has been a journey writing this lecture. At the end, I found myself left with this final thought — to establish gender equality as a fundamental value, we need also to establish care and compassion as values that define the Singaporean. I hope that this lecture has given you much food for thought and look forward to all your questions.

Question-and-Answer Session
Moderated by Ms Lin Suling

Ms Lin Suling: Welcome to the Q&A section of Corinna's second lecture. I am very honoured to be here. Corinna, I first met you at a National Youth Council dialogue. We were on separate panels, but the overall dialogue looked at diversity and inclusion in the workplace. Many big questions were asked. How much of family responsibilities should people leave at the door when they get to work? Is work-life integration a one-way street?

But that was in 2018 and a great deal has happened since then. Not the least, a raging pandemic, and we were reminded of it today when tightened measures were announced — no dining out, group sizes being reduced. So, as the moderator, I will exercise my right to ask you the first question. Could you talk a little bit about COVID-19's impact on women? And looking also at the tightened measures, are there areas of concern we should pay specific attention to? What sort of support do you hope to see in place as well?

Ms Corinna Lim: For COVID-19, it looks like it is going to take some time before we see the end of that. But a few things came out, specifically in relation to women. One is care and how we see care needs in our homes. It has become very clear that a lot of care needs in our day-to-day lives were met because other people were taking care of them. But that's just how essential it is.

Now, it is interesting that things like childcare and eldercare are seen as essential services but are not treated as very important services — we do not even have a Progressive Wage Model (PWM) for these industries. The pay is quite low, especially for eldercare. We had a scheme where we would recruit and train women for childcare and eldercare. A lot more people took up childcare work than eldercare because the pay for childcare workers is higher than eldercare, and it is easier to look after children than the elderly.

For one, we will see these care needs intensify and if we are in lockdown again, it will be a repeat of that situation. Maybe it's better the second time round because we already know what to expect. But we will see those care needs intensify and emerge, including parents who struggle in their homes. The other thing we see is domestic violence — a sharp rise in our helpline calls on domestic violence. Domestic violence is about domination, power and control. And so, when people cannot get out of their homes and the stress is high, it gives rise to a lot more domestic violence. We can expect that again if we have another lockdown. In the current situation, if we can still get out of the house, it may not give rise to so much domestic violence.

Another issue is the work situation for the food and beverage (F&B) industry and industries that have to shut down, especially if workers come from low-income families who have very thin safety nets and hardly any savings. A shutdown for them has huge impacts. The government was great in coming in very quickly, which is one of the things that we hope to see again — that if we get to that situation, can we make sure that an immediate lifeline is there for the people who really need it? And now that we have had some experience with giving this sort of financial support quite quickly, I think the second time will be better. The first time there were people under the self-employed schemes struggling with the forms. There was a lot of confusion — the [network] servers hung and all sorts of things happened. But that was a learning experience. And the government did well in making sure that they were there and were generous enough to support those immediate needs.

Things like eldercare were tricky because community care centres closed. Caregivers at home were suffering because there was no place that they could take their relatives to for the day. Care needs are going to intensify and it is the family members who will have to provide such support. This is where we realise how important it is to have care infrastructure.

Ms Lin: Just to switch gears a little bit and talk about the lecture and the questions that are coming online. Based on your proposal to increase the amount of fathers' leave entitlement to three months, there is a question on why you did not propose the increase of fathers' entitlement to four months, so that it is equal to mothers. Why three?

Ms Lim: I would love to suggest four, but it is not realistic at this point to go from two weeks to four months. I did speak to quite a few people about this, including people who ran small businesses. They questioned, "How will we survive if the men and the women all go on leave?"

We need more things in place first. How do countries that have one-year leave do it? They have a much stronger, much more robust part-time, interim or temporary contract work industry; for every type of industry there is that kind of work and there are people who specialise in matching you when you need a maternity cover. There are people who do this as maternity covers, such as lawyers who are always covering for [others]. We need to have those things in place first. It is a bit of a chicken-and-egg situation. I think if we just did it right now, it would be very difficult.

Funding is also an issue. I have been looking at funding models and interestingly, the best practice is not what we have. The best practice, according to the International Labour Organization (ILO), is something called employment insurance. This is so that the employer does not bear the full burden of giving this leave. Because while the country and the employees want this leave, the employer does not really gain as much. So, they are reluctant. They will do it but they are reluctant. Even to say "can we have eldercare leave for three days?" Ministry of Manpower (MOM) will say "the employers say no, they can't. This year is a bad year, it is already very bad for them in other ways, so we cannot." So, we are sort of held ransom by employers because they cannot afford it.

I think we have to look at different funding models. Employment insurance is such that the employee pays 0.5 or 1 per cent, and the employer pays as well. It funds all leaves, not just parenting leave, but also family leave and leave for single persons. It just goes into this pool and the government also can top up so that it is spread out more. This is so that small companies won't face a big hit to their bottom lines and bear the brunt of paid leave. So, I think we need to look at all these things before we can say four months. As much as I would like to, I think this is what we can manage for now. Even this might be a stretch, but I think we can do it. Because not a lot of men will take all two months, I think it will be a naturally phased approach as people get used to this. But for those who want it, we should go for it.

Ms Lin: Is it a success when more men take leave?

Ms Lim: Yes.

Ms Lin: If so, why not let families choose? Because, ultimately, families are diverse, and the men and women make a decision based on their circumstances.

Ms Lim: The women will still get the same. The women will still get four and the men will get two. Three [for the mother] and three [for the father], I think, some families will do it. But it is more likely that if the men take it, they'll do four [for the mother] and two [for the father]. Because, again, I think women are anchored to the four months already.

Ms Lin: Going back to the intent of this gender equality solution and the ideal we want to reach in having more children and more babies. There is a relevant question here on why we assume that the way to do that is to help women manage caregiving needs for newborns, which reads: Compared to 10 years ago, fewer Singaporean women are getting married, and married women have a TFR that's near replacement. Do you think therefore that the focus should be on encouraging more women to get married instead?

Ms Lim: You're trying to solve the same problem. The people who are not getting married, it's because they don't want to have kids. It's all tied up. It's not necessarily that you treat the two as different pools. You just need to make having a family a very happy thing so that people will get married. Because if you are not planning to have children, you'll probably think, "Okay, getting married or not — if I meet the right guy, that's good, but I'm not actually going to be so active doing it." Then, they focus on their career. So, it's not so different. I think what we're doing now with this proposal is to help people who are not actively thinking of families, because it's so difficult, to start thinking about having one.

Ms Lin: So, it's two pieces of a puzzle?

Ms Lim: I think with this, we are trying to solve the same problem. The main issue is that it is too difficult to have families, so people don't need to get married and are not getting married. Then for the people who are married, are they having the two or three kids that they want to have? I still feel like it is all about making it easier to have children.

Ms Lin: Related to that is a question on how much value we place on home responsibilities and caregiving. Should housewives be compensated for household and caregiving work, which is essentially unpaid labour? How feasible do you think such a policy would be in Singapore?

Ms Lim: This is quite a contentious one, in relation to childcare.

Ms Lin: Why is it contentious?

Ms Lim: It's contentious because we want to encourage women to work — there are many benefits to being able to go out there, work, build your networks and skills. It's a better position for the women at the end of the day. However, some countries have found that when they give this caregiving allowance, many women do choose to become full-time caregivers. It is good to have this choice, but I worry that women who choose to be full-time caregivers might be more vulnerable. The remuneration is usually less than what they get if they go out to work, and they will be less financially secure in the event of a divorce.

I feel differently about eldercare. These are women who are giving up work when they should be building their savings. I feel that for this group, we should seriously consider this proposal — that there is a caregiver allowance. Because we should understand that if we do not do it now, we might have to do it later when they are 70 or 80 and they do not have money. So, it's actually better to just support them now and recognise that they are doing something. If they were not doing it, we would need more nursing homes and infrastructure. All of Singapore wants people to age in place. So as a society, I think we have a justification for this. And the argument that they should be working rather than staying at home does not so much apply to this group, as they have already been working for a long time.

Ms Lin: So what do you make of the discussions last week in Parliament? There was an exchange of views on the Significant Infrastructure Government Loan Act (SINGA) between Deputy Prime Minister Heng Swee Keat and some members of the opposition. The discussion was about whether we should redefine infrastructure to include human capital and social policies. How would you respond to that? And would you make a case for the inclusion of caregiving in infrastructure spending?

Ms Lim: I'm not sure what the significance of making caregiving in Singapore part of infrastructure expenditure is, but I think caregiving is infrastructure. That is my thesis for my lecture. When I say infrastructure, I mean that it is fundamental. Just like education is infrastructure. So yes, it is about services and it's about human capital. I am not sure what the significance is though, if we say it is infrastructure. Does it mean it will have more money? I think what is important is to see it as so fundamental to the health of our economy that we are willing to put more investment into it, knowing that if we do not, the economy and society will suffer.

Ms Lin: There is a question about the "feminisation" of industries and roles that are considered feminine, such as caregiving, education and hospitality. Do you think more needs to be done to address the refusal to give recognition and wages to what is essentially women's work?

Ms Lim: Absolutely. This work is just so devalued. Why is childcare and eldercare so poorly paid? Why is it not on the PWM even though we think of it as essential services? I think there is a pattern of this. That is why I was trying to draw from our childcare experience to our eldercare experience. We just see this sort of undervaluing continue.

Ms Lin: But how do you square off the dilemma that doing so could increase costs for the families we are trying to help?

Ms Lim: Yes, it will increase costs, we have to pay for this. Somehow, we have to fund this. One of the problems is because of the solutions that we have had. With domestic workers, it has completely devalued care. That work now is worth so little because we went for a cheap solution, which has no future. The domestic worker does not build skills that contribute to the economy. If we had not relied on that and we had said that we needed to have professional care, we could have built a professional care industry. But now, we are a little bit hampered by the fact that we have very cheap sources of care. So, a lot of things need to change.

The other thing about the domestic workers solution — not only is it hampering the growth of our other care industries, it is also a very risky thing to rely on the supply of domestic workers, which you ultimately do not control. Foreign governments may impose restrictions or salary controls to reduce the number of their citizens who come to Singapore to work as domestic workers. Also, when these countries start getting more developed, foreign domestic workers may stop being an inexpensive source of caregiving labour.

For example, you want to have your own control over your water supplies because it is basic to life. Similarly, we should try to build a more robust local care infrastructure. If we have to rely on the outside, and we will have to, then let it be higher-end skills that are coming in. We do this for every single other part of our economy, we say we are looking for skills and are very mindful about how many people we let in. But we do not do this for domestic workers, where the controls on the number of domestic workers seem a lot less restrictive than the controls on foreign labour in all other industries. We need to start reducing our dependence on foreign domestic workers. This part needs to be fixed, and it is a structural problem.

Ms Lin: You made a really strong case for the government to invest in this area and double down on the care economy. Therefore, a related question is: In addition to these policy moves that you have already set out, what do you think is the role of businesses and the community in improving the attention and value of the care economy? Or have you given up on the role of the private sector there?

Ms Lim: No, I do not see it as so separate. There are a lot of childcare providers, some are voluntary welfare organisations and some are private. The government funds and controls the standards. It also offers the training institutes and controls a large part of it. However, the business activity is still done by private players. So I think it is important to have both. I certainly do not think that the government should be providing these services — it's way too much. But they should play the role of working with the private sector and determining what needs we have and where we need to grow.

Ms Lin: We have talked a lot about the various aspects of gender equality. This question raises a much larger one, regarding how much of this is about culture. It seems like Singapore's corporate-centric culture and values play a huge part in why some may avoid caregiving work. Singapore's working hours are some of the longest in the world and do not give time for a social or family life. What do you think we can do about that?

Ms Lim: It is absolutely true. We are struggling. That is why I say "caring economy". We need both. I think we are too skewed to the economy and have really neglected the caring part. We need a better balance in society. This goes well beyond the small things. It is about working hours, globalisation, capitalism, neoliberal systems. It just gets faster and more intense. Life 20 years ago, if you remember, I do not know when you started work…

Ms Lin: Yes, I still remember.

Ms Lim: It was slower, right?

Ms Lin: It was different.

Ms Lim: It is so intense now, right?

Ms Lin: We did not have many devices.

Ms Lim: Of course, we did not have those devices that we now never turn off. So how do we deal with this? Some countries have put down rules, like no texts after 8pm. We as a society have to want that. Yes, there is a whole corporate momentum that is hard to stop and I do not know how much people can go on. Climate change, for example, offers a bit of alarm as it is a crisis that is coming up. The young people care more because it is their future. And at some point, this will cause some of us to pause and say, "We cannot go on, it is not sustainable." This is a global issue. That is why I said that Singapore and the world must find some ways of working in a different and more sustainable way.

Ms Lin: Last question: What do you think are the key mindset changes that the government needs to adopt in order for your proposals to be feasible and hopefully implemented? I suppose it is because you have got quite a few to chew on.

Ms Lim: I tried to structure this lecture so that I was not so radical in changing the way the government works, which is a very pragmatic government. There are some limits to it, being pragmatic all the time. I think we have to talk about the values — what caring and dignity means. We have to see it and want it as people.

Regarding a mindset shift for the government, I hope that we have made a compelling case today to say, "Please, do not undervalue care because it is very important for the economy, stability and society in the long-term." For the people, I think we have to start thinking about what is important to our society. When it comes to taxes, for example, if we need to, we pay more tax. That is us paying because we feel these values are important. We want to age well. What is interesting is that the older generation will become the largest cohort of people. They will be the voters of the next elections and will have a say. At the end of the day, I think that it is the people that are needed for fundamental shifts.

Ms Lin: Corinna, thanks so much. It was very nice talking to you.

Lecture III
RESET: MEN, WOMEN, VIOLENCE

W hen we talk about gender equality, the first thing that often comes to mind is that it is mainly a woman's issue — the fight for women's rights. Take for example, the public conversations for the gender equality review. It is titled "Conversations on Singapore Women's Development" and is described as "a national effort to understand Singaporeans' aspirations and ideas on how to further advance our women in Singapore."[1] The unit in the Ministry of Social and Family Development that manages Singapore's compliance with the United Nation's Convention on the Elimination of All Forms of Discrimination Against Women is called the "Office for Women's Development".

I understand why that is the orientation. In a world where men dominate and the default voice and perspective are usually male, women need safe spaces to share their truth and experience. Spaces where they find comfort and support when they have been abused, violated or unfairly treated. And where they can come together to push for a more gender-equal world.

This has been the Association of Women for Action and Research's (AWARE) mission. As a feminist women's rights group, we run a women's

---

[1] REACH, "Conversations on Singapore Women's Development," accessed May 20, 2021, https://www.reach.gov.sg/en/Participate/conversations-on-singapore-womens-development.

helpline, counselling, support groups and the Sexual Assault Care Centre. We focus on the women's perspective — as career women, family caregivers, single mothers, migrant spouses, mothers in low-income families and survivors of gender violence. The work never ends.

However, we will not ever solve misogyny, gender discrimination, violence and exploitation if, as a society, we do not deal with the issues that men face as men. My work involves focusing on women and prior to this lecture series, I had not gone too deeply into understanding men's experiences.

What is it like for men living in a world that expects them to be the breadwinner? To always be strong, powerful, self-reliant, stoic and dominant? The script for what it means to be a man in Singapore is fast changing, driven mainly by women's empowerment and their expanded role in society. The change is good. We have to keep moving towards equal opportunities for all.

The patriarchal system accords men with higher status, more power, money and opportunities. But it comes at a very high cost. We need to understand what it is in the system that makes it hard for men to change, even though they may not find the situation ideal. Going forward, I hope that men will understand how patriarchy hurts us all, including men, and will want to join the gender equality movement. To grow beyond the constraints of patriarchy, men need encouragement and support.

In this lecture, I will focus on men and masculinity in Singapore. What are the norms that shape their psyche and patterns of behaviour? I will also make suggestions for what we can do to support men in embracing a more gender-equal mindset. Finally, I will discuss how we can best educate and protect our next generation of men and women who are growing up in a hyper-sexualised world.

Social Constructs

There has not been much research on the topic of masculinity in Singapore. In fact, that topic is fairly new in the world. Women's studies began much earlier because of the systemic oppression of women. In 1949, Simone de

Beauvoir's iconic study of women, *The Second Sex*, elegantly captured the women's condition in this famous line:

> *One is not born, but rather becomes, a woman.*

In other words, femininity is a social construct. Biology does not determine what makes a woman, a woman. A woman learns her role from society.

Simone de Beauvoir was way ahead of her time. *The Second Sex* went on to inspire generations of feminist work. Today, science has caught up. Brain scientists now understand that human brains are extremely plastic and malleable. As babies, our brains start off soft as clay. As we grow up, our brains are changed by our life experiences — jobs, hobbies, social messages that we receive. Over time, these repeated actions and messages get wired into the brain's network.[2]

Take girls for example — the pink dolls that they play with, the fairy tales of princesses being saved by Prince Charming, the many messages girls receive to be sweet and agreeable. These mould and shape their brains. Again, as de Beauvoir said, one is not born but becomes a woman.

Knowing that gender is a social construct has been extremely empowering for women. Women realised they could, and so they began to change the script handed down to them by society. The main resistance to this change has been, and here is where de Beauvoir's next most famous line comes in:

> *The problem of women has always been a problem of men.*

To be clear, men themselves are not the problem. The problem is one of masculine norms. The social construct that makes men, men. To borrow the words of de Beauvoir, in the context of men:

> *One is not born, but rather becomes, a man.*

---

[2] Gina Rippon, *The Gendered Brain: The New Neuroscience that Shatters the Myth of the Female Brain* (London: The Bodley Head, 2019).

So, what are the masculine norms that define men's lives in Singapore? If these norms are a problem, what needs to change?

Men and Masculinity

As there is not much research in this area, I carried out my own survey in the form of a dozen interviews with men. The men I interviewed fell into three main groups:

1) Men who had not thought too much about gender issues
2) Men who bucked the male stereotype
3) Men who have run support groups for men

This section is based on whatever research I could find, my own personal experiences and these interviews. Although anecdotal, it does provide some good starting points for further discussion.

Let us start with a definition of masculine norms: Masculine norms are beliefs that define what are acceptable and appropriate thoughts, feelings and actions for men. They are embedded in formal and informal institutions, nested in the mind and produced and reproduced through social interaction. They play a role in shaping women and men's (often unequal) access to resources and freedoms, thus affecting their voice, power and sense of self.[3]

Globally, the work on masculine norms started only in the 1980s. A few psychometric measures have been created to assess the strengths of these norms. As far as I know, there is no research on the application of these measures in Singapore. Here is a list of masculine norms from a well-established psychometric measure known as the Conformity to Masculine Norms Inventory.[4] There are nine norms on this list.

---

[3] Adapted from Beniamino Cislaghi and Lori Heise, "Gender Norms and Social Norms: Differences, Similarities and Why they Matter in Prevention Science," *Sociology of Health & Illness* 42, no. 2 (2020): 415–16; Ronald Levant, "Moving Beyond Toxic Masculinity: A Q&A with Ronald Levant," *Oxford University Press Blog*, May 30, 2020, https://blog.oup.com/2020/05/moving-beyond-toxic-masculinity-a-qa-with-ronald-levant.

[4] Adapted from Mike C. Parent and Bonnie Moradi, "Confirmatory Factor Analysis of the Conformity to Masculine Norms Inventory and Development of the Conformity to Masculine Norms Inventory-46," *Psychology of Men & Masculinity* 10, no. 3 (2009): 176.

Some of these norms have been recognised as harmful or toxic in that they inhibit men's ability to be emotionally vulnerable and form deep connections in adult relationships, contribute to sexist, misogynistic and homophobic behaviours, gender violence and aggression.[5] The term "toxic masculinity" does not mean that men are inherently toxic, but that they face expectations to behave in ways that may be harmful to themselves or to others.

I have divided these norms into two categories: those that are generally harmful or toxic, and those that are harmful if they are practised in a more extreme way (Table 1).

Table 1.   Masculine norms

Toxic	Non-toxic, if not extreme
1) Emotional Control	7) Winning
2) Risk-Taking	8) Self-Reliance
3) Power over Women	9) Primacy of Work
4) Playboy Behaviour	
5) Violence	
6) Heterosexual Self-Presentation	

Let me briefly explain the "non-toxic, if not extreme" indicators. It is good to have a level of desire to win, for example. This in itself is not toxic. However, what is toxic is if you try to win at all costs. This list gave me a good way of making sense of the men's stories that I will be sharing today. These norms shape men's lives by the effect it has on them and those around them.

Dad's Story

Let me first share the story of the man whom I know best, whom I love and respect: my dad, Francis, who passed last year just after his 82nd birthday.

---

[5] American Psychological Association, Boys and Men Guidelines Group, "APA Guidelines for Psychological Practice with Boys and Men," August 2018, https://www.apa.org/about/policy/boys-men-practice-guidelines.pdf.

He was born in the late 1930s, just before the war. I think of him as the typical pioneer generation man. Hardworking, reliable, disciplined family man with conservative views. He married my mum, June, an intelligent, strong-willed, independent woman. Together, they had me, my twin and my youngest sister.

Gender-wise, Dad was constantly outnumbered in the family. Four women to one man. Dad was a good man. He loved his family and worked very hard to make sure that all his daughters had a good start to life. He loved sports and coached us to be competitive tennis and squash players.

In terms of the Conformity to Masculine Norms Inventory assessment, he would have scored very high on:

- Primacy of Work
- Emotional control
- Self-reliance

Dad took his role as breadwinner and protector very seriously. Work came first and then family. Outside work, Dad spent a lot of time with the family. Most conversations when we were young centred on school and tennis, and then later, on our professional lives. Sometimes we talked politics but that could get a bit heated. He was extremely stoic. Never talked about his feelings or problems and did not know how to connect with me and my sisters emotionally. Likewise, even though we loved and respected him, we were not close to him.

When Dad retired at 60, he fell into a deep depression. Like many men, his life revolved around work. Without it, he was lost. The few friends he had were his colleagues. After he retired, the friendships waned. Dad was depressed for a few years.

For me, the saddest part of this story is that although we lived together in the same flat, I had no idea that he was having a hard time. We were just so disconnected. I only found out about his depression a few years later, after my mother told me about it. At which point, I was crushed. How could I be so blind and oblivious to his pain and humanity? My dad did everything he was supposed to do as a good man, including repressing his emotions and being self-reliant. Dad never knew this, but he is one of the reasons why I do this work, championing gender equality. It breaks my heart to think that most men have to live as Dad did — locked in a prison of masculinity.

I am happy to say that this story has a good ending. Although Dad had many health conditions, he was blessed with longevity. Perhaps, growing old, having nothing left to prove and knowing we are all living on borrowed time helped him transform. He became a totally different man when he broke out of his masculine jail in the last 10 years of his life. He became comfortable with himself, laughed easily and was fun to be around. Every day was precious to him. He made it a point to tell mum and his girls how much he loved us and how proud he was of us. He shared his reflections of life, including his regrets.

One sweet memory of Dad that I will always keep in my heart is him lying on the bed, holding my hand and telling me about his various trips to the oncologist. He would hold my hand for a long time. I will forever feel my dad's loving touch. Dad passed away in his sleep. The way he wanted to go, without bothering anyone. I believe that Dad died well, with love and peace in his heart.

Prison of Masculinity

This is an illustration of the prison of masculinity (Figure 1). Many men are still trapped in this prison.

My dad was lucky. He had an extra 20 years to find himself and to live a much fuller life. Not every man who is trapped in the prison of masculinity will have that chance. For those dads who are reading this and feeling like they might have some breaking out to do, please start right away. Go to your kids, give them a big hug and tell them you love them.

It will not be easy to break out because the norms of masculinity are often reinforced by other men, women and the structures of the world we

Figure 1.   The prison of masculinity

Source: Mithalina Taib for the Institute of Policy Studies

live in. Also, the rest of society have become very used to how men are, using phrases like "boys will be boys" and "men have egos".

But there are some glimmers of hope. I believe that change will happen once men begin to see how much they have to gain when they get out of their prison. I also hope more men's groups will be formed and become active like the women's movement. Women's groups cannot do this work for men, but you will have our full support.

Dominance and Violence

Let us move on to the theme of dominance and violence. Almost all the men that I interviewed spoke about dominance over other men or boys. About having to be the alpha male, whether it was being good at sports, studies or becoming an officer in National Service (NS). One had to distinguish oneself and win friends in doing so.

The pressure to prove their manhood is constant. It is a game of dominance — having to keep being better, stronger, faster and more successful than the next man. Women do not face the same pressures. The dark side of this dominance is violence. This came up much more than I had expected before I started my interviews. I was surprised and disturbed by the level of violence, bullying, assault, pain and humiliation that boys and young men inflict on one another. This shows up in statistics as well as in my interviews.

Tim's Story

By the time Tim was 14, he had a few incidents of harassment and bullying that made his school life miserable. These are two of his stories. They include some pretty graphic details that are necessary to illustrate the point.

Tim attended an all-boys school. When he was in Secondary One, there was a well-known bully in his class. As a transfer student from another country, the bully was three years older and much bigger than all the other kids in class. One day, when Tim went to the toilet, this older boy attacked Tim and stuck a finger into Tim's anus. It was painful and humiliating, but Tim did not report this incident to anyone. He said, "It didn't occur to me that reporting was something I could or should do. Not to a teacher, not to my parents. It was a shameful thing that had to be brushed off or buried."

Tim was not a physically "wimpy" kind of guy. In fact, Tim was a national school swimmer. He would go every day to Toa Payoh Swimming Complex to train with other national swimmers, swimming 5 to 6 kilometres on school days and double that during holidays.

One day, after a training session, when all the swimmers were cooling down, an older boy wrapped his legs around Tim in the pool, kept him in a lock and peed on him. It was not only an act of bullying but a performance for the entertainment of the bully's clique. Tim was humiliated. But again, there was nothing to be said about it. As Tim said, "It was a ragging that had to be endured."

Incidents like this made Tim very uncomfortable with jock cultures and all-male cliques that he saw around him. As an adult, Tim would struggle with depression and rage and all the attendant problems of alcoholism and self-harm. He said, "I don't think my depression can be attributed wholly to childhood bullying and assault, but certainly those events played a major role in shaping my rather dim view of human society, and a sense that one had to combat aggression with aggression."

I am grateful to Tim for sharing his stories of sexual assault and bullying. We do not hear these stories often. Men rarely report these things or seek help because such confessions would violate the masculine norms that "real men don't show their hurt" and should not cry. When faced with adversity, men should just "suck it up" and get on with things. At 13, Tim was already well socialised as a young boy to be stoic and not to betray weakness.

Prevalence of Bullying and Gender Policing

We have a very serious school bullying issue in Singapore. A 2015 Organisation for Economic Co-operation and Development (OECD) study showed that 15-year-olds in Singapore experienced more bullying than their peers in 52 other countries. We are the third highest after New Zealand and Latvia. Nearly 15 per cent of Singapore students described being frequently bullied. That is one and a half in 10.[6]

What is more worrying and salient to this lecture is the high level of social pressure in schools to make boys conform to norms of masculinity — what we call "gender policing". AWARE's 2017 survey shows that nine in 10 teenage boys faced social pressures to be "manly" through teasing, harassment, bullying and social exclusion. They were told to "man up" and to "take it like a man". Those considered to have feminine characteristics were called "sissy", "*pondan*", "*ah kua*" or "gay".

---

[6] Yuen Sin, "Singapore Has Third Highest Rate of Bullying Globally: Study," *The Straits Times*, August 20, 2017, https://www.straitstimes.com/singapore/education/republic-has-third-highest-rate-of-bullying-globally.

Boys who were pressured to conform to masculine norms were four times more likely to commit violence against others. In other words, violence breeds violence.

Peer Pressure

Peer pressure is a powerful influencer. A few men I interviewed said that they were part of all-male chat groups where some men would regularly send sexual messages or images that objectify women. These WhatsApp chat groups were either professionally connected, former classmates or army mates. Some of these professionally connected groups involve men at senior levels of management.

The interviewees said that although they did not themselves circulate these sexual texts or messages, neither did they call out this behaviour. It is important to note that the men I interviewed were all decent, respectable, capable and thoughtful men.

The interviewees gave three reasons for not taking action:

1) It was pointless. Their speaking up would not stop this.
2) They would lose social capital.
3) They thought it was harmless and that the men who sent the messages were not bad men who would hurt women.

Speaking up against toxic acts of masculinity is very difficult in a group setting. The person who steps up and calls it out risks losing his hard-won masculinity. My interviewees understood that masculinity is what psychologists have described as precarious — hard to win and easy to lose.[7] So, they do not speak up.

As for the idea that "locker room" exchanges are harmless, what do you think? Going back to brain science, repeated locker room banter shapes and moulds the brain. Even if men do not consciously think they

---

[7] Joseph A. Vandello, Jennifer K. Bosson, Dov Cohen, Rochelle M. Burnaford, and Jonathan R. Weaver, "Precarious Manhood," *Journal of Personal Social Psychology* 95, no. 6 (December 2008): 1328.

have less respect for women, as a result of hearing these kinds of conversations, their brains are making associations. It is not harmless.

Masculine Norms, Bullying and Gender Violence

So, what is the link between toxic masculinity, bullying and gender violence? Research has shown a close link between school bullying and gender violence:

- Young boys who engaged in bullying were much more likely to engage in sexual harassment of the other sex as teenagers.[8]
- Childhood bullying was also correlated to intimate partner violence among young adults and domestic violence.[9]

It is also well established that toxic masculinity norms are at the root of violence against women.[10] The implications of this are that if we are to prevent or reduce gender violence, we must:

1) Engage men and boys
2) Reduce bullying
3) Promote positive masculine norms

---

[8] Dorothy L. Espelage, Kathleen C. Basile, and Merle E. Hamburger, "Bullying Perpetration and Subsequent Sexual Violence Perpetration Among Middle School Students," *Journal of Adolescent Health* 50, no. 1 (2012): 64–65; Dorothy L. Espelage, Kathleen C. Basile, Lisa De La Rue, and Merle E. Hamburger, "Longitudinal Associations Among Bullying, Homophobic Teasing, and Sexual Violence Perpetration Among Middle School Students," *Journal of Interpersonal Violence* 30, no. 14 (2015): 2554–55; Dorothy L. Espelage, Kathleen C. Basile, Ruth W. Leemis, Tracy N. Hipp, and Jordan P. Davis, "Longitudinal Examination of the Bullying-Sexual Violence Pathway Across Early to Late Adolescence: Implicating Homophobic Name-Calling," *Journal of Youth and Adolescence* 47, no. 9 (2018): 1881–82.

[9] Jennifer Connolly, Debra Pepler, Wendy Craig, and Ali Taradash, "Dating Experiences of Bullies in Early Adolescence," *Child Maltreatment* 5, no. 4 (2000): 306–8; Dorothy L. Espelage, Sabina Low, Carolyn Anderson, and Lisa De La Rue, "Relation Between Bully & Teen Dating Violence Perpetration Across Early to Late Adolescence," Press release, August, 2018, https://www.apa.org/news/press/releases/2013/08/bully-dating.pdf; Benjamin D. Locke and James R. Mahalik, "Examining Masculinity Norms, Problem Drinking, and Athletic Involvement as Predictors of Sexual Aggression in College Men," *Journal of Counseling Psychology* 52, no. 3 (2005): 281–82; Joan Arehart-Treichel, "Childhood Bullying Correlates With Adult Domestic Violence," *Psychiatric News* 47, no. 1 (2012): 12–13.

[10] Juan Herrero, Andrea Torres, Francisco J. Rodríguez, and Joel Juarros-Basterretxea, "Intimate Partner Violence Against Women in the European Union: The Influence of Male Partners' Traditional Gender Roles and General Violence," *Psychology of Violence* 7, no. 3 (2017): 390–91; Moira Carmody, Michael Salter, and Geir Henning Presterudstuen, *Less to Lose and More to Gain? Men and Boys Violence Prevention Research Project: Final Report* (Australia: University of Western Sydney, 2014); M. Christina Santana, Anita Raj, Michele R. Decker, Ana La Marche, and Jay G. Silverman, "Masculine Gender Roles Associated with Increased Sexual Risk and Intimate Partner Violence Perpetration Among Young Adult Men," *Journal of Urban Health* 83, no. 4 (2006): 581–82.

While there have been ad hoc campaigns like AWARE's White Ribbon Campaign where men take a stand against gender violence on November 25, the International Day to End Violence Against Women, there has not been any sustained work to engage men and boys.

National Service and Other Policies That Apply Only to Men

No lecture on masculinities in Singapore would be complete without an examination of NS. It is also a relevant matter when it comes to gender equality. Research carried out for AWARE by Internet research company, Quilt Ai, showed that across the major social media platforms, NS is the number one reason that men assert to oppose gender equality in Singapore.

This section on NS is based on the limited research available on NS and the accounts of men that I interviewed for this lecture. NS is the hallmark of Singaporean masculinity. It is the national rite of passage every Singaporean boy goes through to become a man.[11] The men whom I spoke to described NS as a hyper-masculine experience. After all, it is designed to toughen up our boys and build bonds between males across ethnic and class divides.

However, there are aspects of NS that bring out the more negative norms of masculinity. The exclusion of women, the use of homophobic and misogynistic insults like "gay", "faggot", "sissy" and "*gu niang*", and the constant shaming and humiliation by superiors for minor infractions create an atmosphere that many people today would describe as "toxic masculinity".

This environment gives rise to:

- "Blanket parties" where the group turns against one soldier who is perceived to be the weakest link or is disliked. They throw a blanket over him and rain blows on him.
- Soldiers talking about sex a lot. Like sharing prurient details about sexual intercourse with their girlfriends or organising trips to Geylang with their buddies after booking out.

---

[11] John Lowe, "Masculinizing National Service: The Cultural Reproduction of Masculinities and Militarization of Male Citizenship in Singapore," *Journal of Gender Studies* 28, no. 6 (2019): 695–96.

Here is how my youngest interviewee, who is still in NS, described how men interacted:

> *Predatory behaviour is almost encouraged — everyone's favourite subject is girls. Dates, Tinder matches, looking up women on Instagram.*
>
> *Creeping is also quite blatant. If anyone mentions they have a sister, the inevitable follow-up is something along the lines of: Is she pretty? Can I get her number? Is she single? Does she have a boyfriend?*
>
> *This kind of image of a man as an uncontrollable monster who just needs sex is constantly normalised.*

I find it disturbing that the rite of passage of manhood in Singapore is one that involves such toxic masculinity norms and practices.

Other Reasons for Focusing on Masculine Norms

Unhealthy masculine norms are also linked to suicide, crime and substance abuse. Men's suicide rate is double that of women's in Singapore as well as in most other countries.[12] It is interesting that research often shows that men suffer less depression than women. Yet, their suicide rates are actually higher.[13]

Former Senior Assistant Director of the Samaritans of Singapore, Ms Wong Lai Chun, explained that this is largely due to the fact that "men tend to compare themselves to a standard masculine role that emphasises strength, independence and risk-taking behaviour. They feel continual pressure to solve issues on their own and to suppress feelings of distress."[14]

---

[12] Sue-Ann Cheow, "Men Twice as Likely to Commit Suicide," *The New Paper*, April 29, 2019, https://www.tnp.sg/news/singapore/men-twice-likely-commit-suicide.

[13] Kelly Ng, "S'pore Women More Likely to Suffer From Depression Than Men: IMH Study," *Today*, December 4, 2017, https://www.todayonline.com/singapore/spore-women-more-likely-suffer-depression-men-imh-study.

[14] Cheow, "Men Twice as Likely to Commit Suicide."

In Singapore, 83 per cent of drug abusers are men and 90 per cent of inmates are men.[15] Research has shown that the higher rates of crime and drug abuse by men are also linked to masculine norms.[16] Masculinities' expert Michael Flood says, "The rate of violence and crime committed by men reflects very long-standing dominant traits of masculinity that come from how we socialise men and boys to dominate, take risks and refrain from empathy."[17]

Understanding masculine norms and engaging with men and boys with this lens offers much potential for advancing gender equality, improving men's health and reducing crime and substance abuse rates. Knowing that masculinity is a social script that can be changed, there is much scope and need to change negative masculine norms. Governments, parents, schools, workplaces and community groups all have a role to play.

My Recommendations

I have three main policy recommendations on what we can do to take things forward in relation to:

a) Engaging men and boys regarding gender equality.
b) Promoting positive masculine norms.

Recommendation 1: Commission a Study on Men and Boys as Part of the Gender Equality Review

Masculine norms affect men's development, their interactions with women and their engagement in the family. Masculinity is both a part of the problem and the solution to gender equality. Thus, my first recommendation is for

---

[15] Ministry of Home Affairs, Central Narcotics Bureau, "Demographic Profile of Drug Abusers," accessed May 20, 2021, https://data.gov.sg/dataset/demographic-profile-of-drug-abusers?resource_id=81181cb9-71e4-4a01-b4e2-26; Ministry of Home Affairs, Singapore Prison Service, "Convicted Penal Population," accessed May 20, 2021, https://data.gov.sg/dataset/convicted-penal-inmates-population?view_id=c8ab3504-6e16-4314-8c91-2b7298154c84&resource_id=7070dc26-a95a-4560-8670-6682705a9cff.

[16] Steven J. Lash, Michael M. Copenhaver, and Richard M. Eisler, "Masculine Gender Role Stress and Substance Abuse Among Substance Dependent Males," *Journal of Gender, Culture, and Health* 3, no. 3 (1998): 188–90.

[17] Jane Gilmore, "We Know Violence, Crime and Masculinity are Linked. It's Time to Look at Why, and How to Stop It," *The Sydney Morning Herald*, October 19, 2017, https://www.smh.com.au/lifestyle/we-know-violence-crime-and-masculinity-are-linked-its-time-to-look-at-why-and-how-to-stop-it-20171019-gz3zq3.html.

the government to commission a study on masculinity, men and boys, as part of the gender equality review. We need to understand masculinity in Singapore and its implications on gender equality.

The study should include an action plan on how we engage with men and boys to promote healthy masculine norms in Singapore. It should cover the areas of:

- Equality in the family
- Intimate partner relationships
- Health and well-being

Many Western countries like the United Kingdom, Australia, Canada and organisations like the United Nations (UN) have started to actively focus on men and masculinities.

In 2019, the UK government commissioned an in-depth study on this and issued a report titled "Changing Gender Norms: Engaging with Men and Boys". There are many interesting nuggets, findings and recommendations in the UK report. First, they found that the belief that some men and boys have about their entitlement to sex and control in relationships could lead to aggression when these ideas are challenged. Second, they found that it was important to use a strengths-based approach. For example, to broaden the idea of masculine strength to include tenderness or caring for a child. Third, that there is no one masculinity. It has to be, as with feminism, an intersectional approach. We need to look at the masculine norms across religion, social class, sexual orientation and ageing men (especially for their health issues).

The Canadian government in 2018 set aside CAD$1.8 million in order to engage men on masculinity issues.[18] At this point, I think that a study on masculinity is the priority, but if there are resources, the study should also include a study on feminine norms.

---

[18] Government of Canada, "Backgrounder — The Government of Canada Invests in Engaging Men and Boys in Gender Equality," November 26, 2020, https://www.canada.ca/en/women-gender-equality/news/2019/08/backgrounder--the-government-of-canada-invests-in-engaging-men-and-boys-in-gender-equality.html.

Recommendation 2: Initiate or Support the Establishment of Dedicated Support Services for Men

A few of the men I interviewed spoke about the need for specialised services to support men who are facing stress and challenges in their lives. Men face a lot of pressure to conform to the norms and expectations that society places on them, including the pressure to be successful at work, to be strong, to not show their vulnerability or to ask for help.

The dearth of dedicated men's support services in Singapore makes it even more difficult for men to access help when they are facing a crisis such as unemployment, marital difficulties or being caught for a sexual offence.

My recommendation, based on discussions with counsellors and men who work with men, is for the government to initiate or support the setting up of dedicated men's services like a men's helpline (to make it easy and safe for people to contact them), coaching (not counselling) and men's groups (not support groups). We need to design services to take into account masculine norms that make it difficult for men to seek help.

The aim of the men's services is to provide a non-judgmental, non-shaming, hope-giving environment that acknowledges men's painful experiences. It will be a space:

- Where men can allow themselves to be vulnerable and not experience it as weakness or shame.
- Where they can work through their vulnerabilities and discover strengths in themselves and hope for the future.
- Where they can gain healthy acceptance of the good men that they are instead of constantly being disappointed by not being able to measure up to unrealistic masculine norms.

A lot of masculinity is about being accepted by other men. Well-facilitated men's support groups have a lot to offer.

Bryan Tan, who helms Dads for Life, shared about the excellent work that the organisation was doing.[19] Within the safe space of small all-male

---

[19] Bryan Tan, personal communication with Corinna Lim, February 22, 2021.

groups, men would share honestly about their parenting struggles and concerns. They have more than a hundred of such men's groups.

The high number of Dads for Life groups is a sign of the effectiveness of these supportive all-male groups. We need a range of such groups to support men on different issues. For example, groups for men contemplating divorce, men dealing with infidelity, men facing abuse, and men with compulsive sexual fetishes.

Recommendation 3: Review National Service — Promote Positive Masculine Norms and Make National Service Gender Equal

I have two major recommendations in relation to NS.

The first more immediate-term recommendation is to review NS to eliminate all practices that promote sexism, misogyny and homophobia, and to use NS as an opportunity to promote positive norms.

The men I interviewed said that the most problematic aspects of NS, in relation to promoting unhealthy masculine norms, were the parts that related to Basic Military Training (BMT) and vocational training.

The units that NS men were posted to after their initial training had much less sexism, misogyny and homophobia, and showed that discipline could be instilled in a professional way without resorting to these negative practices.

The official line may be that the authorities do not condone sexism, misogyny and homophobia, but this is still quite prevalent in practice.

There is much scope for NS to reduce negative norms of sexism, misogyny and homophobia. In fact, NS presents a golden opportunity to actively role model and promote positive norms of respect and equality among young men.

In the longer term, if NS continues to exist, despite the calls to abolish it, I hope that the government will consider expanding the scope of NS beyond the military and making the expanded NS gender neutral.

For gender equality to be fully realised in Singapore, we have to work towards a situation where both women and men have equal opportunity and responsibility to serve the country. Aside from promoting equality, Singapore's changing demographics provide compelling reasons for us to expand NS to include community, social and healthcare services, and to require women to serve NS.

First, our population is shrinking, and the number of male conscripts is set to decrease by about a third by 2030.[20]

Second, the expansion of NS to include non-military service will help us to meet the increased social, health and care needs of an ageing population.

This is not a new idea. My S R Nathan Fellow predecessor Mr Ho Kwon Ping had suggested that in anticipation of a time when Singapore may in fact need women in military defence, we should take the first step of conscripting all women to do five months of healthcare and social care work.[21]

I think it is possible to start as Mr Ho suggested — that all women are conscripted and can choose either two-year NS in the Singapore Armed Forces (SAF), Singapore Police Force (SPF) or Singapore Civil Defence Force (SCDF). Or they can choose five months of healthcare or social care work. But ultimately, we should make NS totally gender-neutral so that everyone, regardless of gender, can opt for two years military, police, civil defence, community or healthcare and other Total Defence areas that need people.

Youth, Sex and the Internet

This next part of the lecture will deal with youth, sex and the Internet.

Pornography is now widely available on the Internet. We do not know how widely it is used in Singapore. A search on SimilarWeb for the top-visited websites here showed that one adult site was ranked 11th, ahead of Netflix, Reddit, WhatsApp and LinkedIn.[22] What is alarming is that our boys are exposed to porn from an early age.

---

[20] Ashton Ng Jing Kai, "Not Justified to Use NS to Teach Women Graciousness," *Today*, November 14, 2019, https://www.todayonline.com/voices/not-justified-use-ns-teach-women-graciousness.

[21] Kwon Ping Ho, *The Ocean in a Drop: Singapore: The Next Fifty Years* (Singapore: World Scientific, 2015), 67.

[22] SimilarWeb, "Top Websites Ranking in Singapore," accessed May 20, 2021, https://www.similarweb.com/top-websites/singapore.

Nine out of every 10 teenage boys between 13 and 15 years old watched or read sexually explicit materials in 2015, according to a survey done by Touch Cyber Wellness.[23] More than half of them intentionally sought it out. Some were exposed to it even before they started primary school.

In contrast, only 8 per cent of girls — less than one in 10 — said they viewed pornography, either intentionally or by accident. What is also worrying is the type of porn that is available on the most accessible sites. A recent study that reviewed over 150,000 titles on the three most popular porn sites in the UK found that one in eight titles shown to first-time users on the first page of mainstream porn sites contained depictions of sexual violence.[24] The most common form of sexual violence depicted was sexual activity between immediately family members, with fathers and mothers being the perpetrators. Physical aggression and sexual assault came next — women being gagged, choked and slapped. The third highest was images taken or uploaded without consent, including revenge porn, upskirting and images taken by hidden cameras.

In the past, there have been concerns that porn would lead to more rapes. But there is no clear evidence of this. However, that does not mean that porn consumption and addiction are harmless. Let us examine what the research does show about the consumption of porn by men and boys.

Most mass-market pornography conveys the belief that sex is divorced from intimacy and that women are always ready for sex.[25] This often leads to men being dissatisfied with their own sex lives. Research shows that men who watched violent porn were more than six times as likely to have engaged

---

[23] Janice Tai, "Nine in 10 Teen Boys in Singapore Exposed to Porn: Survey," *The Straits Times*, June 29, 2016, https://www.straitstimes.com/singapore/nine-in-10-teen-boys-exposed-to-porn-survey.

[24] Fiona Vera-Gray, Clare McGlynn, Ibad Kureshi, and Kate Butterby, "Sexual Violence as a Sexual Script in Mainstream Online Pornography," *The British Journal of Criminology* 61, no. 3 (2021): 7–12.

[25] Gail Dines, Robert Jensen, and Ann Russo, *Pornography: The Production and Consumption of Inequality* (New York: Routledge, 1998), 72.

in sexually aggressive behaviour.[26] Increased use of porn by adolescents predicted more sexist attitudes and perpetration of sexual harassment two years later.[27]

What should be our biggest concern? The fact is that many young people are turning to porn as their default sex educator. A study of 18- to 24-year-olds in the United States found that a quarter of them listed porn as their most helpful source of sex information.[28] Porn sex is not like real sex, but people are still using porn as their education on real sex. Porn is not going to go away. It is pervasive.

Thus, the only effective antidote is education. To put pornography into the right context so that young people understand that what they see is a fantasy and does not represent healthy, consensual relationships. Humiliation, shaming or scare tactics do not work. They drive porn-watching behaviour into the shadows, thereby denying educators and parents the opportunity to counter unhealthy ideas that porn may be seeding in young minds.

Sex Education in Singapore

What we need is good sex education. So, let us pause for a moment to consider: Whose role is it to carry out sex education? Who should be the primary sex educator in Singapore? Is it the school? Or is it parents? The Ministry of Education (MOE) says parents are in charge. The MOE website says:

> *As parents, you play a primary role in your child's Sexuality Education. No matter where they get their information from, you are the best person to teach them what is right or wrong.*[29]

---

[26] Michele L. Ybarra, Kimberly J. Mitchell, Merle Hamburger, Marie Diener-West, and Philip J. Leaf, "X-Rated Material and Perpetration of Sexually Aggressive Behavior Among Children and Adolescents: Is There a Link?" *Aggressive Behavior* 37, no. 1 (2011): 14–15.

[27] Jane D. Brown and Kelly L. L'Engle, "X-Rated: Sexual Attitudes and Behaviors Associated with U.S. Early Adolescents' Exposure to Sexually Explicit Media," *Communication Research* 36, no. 1 (2009): 142–44.

[28] Michelle Samuels, "Porn Isn't There to Teach You What You Are Supposed to Do When You Are Having Sex," *Boston University School of Public Health*, January 6, 2021, https://www.bu.edu/sph/news/articles/2021/young-adults-say-pornography-main-source-of-info.

[29] Ministry of Education, "Sexuality Education: Roles of Stakeholders," accessed May 20, 2021, https://www.moe.gov.sg/programmes/sexuality-education/stakeholders.

Do parents actually live up to this role? No, they do not. AWARE's 2018 survey showed that seven out of 10 youths did not talk to their parents about sex. A second survey with parents showed that they knew that it was their responsibility to talk to their kids about sex, but only 50 per cent of parents were comfortable to do so.[30] Given that many parents do not know how to have frank discussions with their children, schools should then play a bigger role.

Effectiveness of School Sex Education

Let us look at how effective our schools' sex education programme has been so far. AWARE has been tracking this for many years. The feedback from youths has been consistently negative. A 2019 article on MOE's Sex Education programme in *Today* contained this response from a student about the programme:

> *They keep talking about abstinence and how we should not have sex. It's not wrong, but I think with young people, the more you tell us not to do something, the more we want to do it because we were at the age to try out different things.*[31]

Another article in the well-known millennial website, the Millennials of Singapore website, says that the MOE programme is unrealistic:[32]

> *Teens are having sex, and it's silly for anyone to think otherwise. That makes it all the more crucial that teens are provided with necessary information to help them in making informed choices.*
> *Rather than trying to prevent the impossible i.e. teenagers having sex and living with the idealistic mindset that teens will abstain till marriage, schools should address the obvious straight on.*

---

[30] AWARE, "Only Half of Parents Are Comfortable Talking to Their Kids About Sex Ed, While Most Prefer School Programmes to Focus on Consent Over Abstinence: AWARE-Blackbox Survey," July 1, 2020, https://www.aware.org.sg/2020/07/parents-comfortable-sex-ed-consent-abstinence-aware-blackbox-survey.

[31] Nabilah Awang and Tessa Oh, "Let's Talk About Safe Sex: Sex Education Should Go Beyond Preaching Abstinence, Say Students and Experts," *Today*, October 28, 2019, https://www.todayonline.com/singapore/lets-talk-about-safe-sex-sex-education-should-go-beyond-preaching-abstinence-say-students.

[32] Anmol Vaswani, "Is There a Need for Better Sex Education That's More Than STDs and Abstinence?" *Millennials of SG*, August 19, 2018, https://mosg.tv/2018/08/19/is-there-a-need-for-better-sex-education-thats-more-than-stds-and-abstinence.

It's time sex education lessons started giving students answers to questions that they shouldn't be looking for on Google.

What is MOE's approach to Sex Education?

Sexuality Education in schools promotes abstinence before marriage, and teaches facts about contraception, consequences of casual sex, prevention of diseases, and how to say "no" to sexual advances.[33]

Is abstinence before marriage realistic considering that people here tie the knot much later these days — 29 for women and 30 for men? AWARE's recent focus group discussions on sex education affirm the earlier youths' views that school sex education is inadequate. The group shared two issues:

1) The topic of pornography is either avoided altogether or dismissed as taboo.

2) There is not enough discussion about youths engaging in activities like sexting and cases where intimate photographs are shared without consent.

One problem is that there is not much public data and research available. We have seen an increase in media reports on voyeurism, upskirting and non-consensual sharing of young women's intimate photos, many of these involving incidents on campuses. In the last four years, AWARE saw a tripling of sexual violence cases facilitated by technology.[34]

Recommendation 4: To Initiate or Support Research on Youths' Sex Education Needs

So, as part of the gender equality review, I urge the government to initiate or support research to find out more about the sexual behaviour and educational needs of our youths today.

---

[33] Ministry of Education, "Sexuality Education: Scope and Teaching Approach," accessed May 20, 2021, https://www.moe.gov.sg/programmes/sexuality-education/scope-and-teaching-approach.

[34] AWARE, "AWARE's Sexual Assault Care Centre Saw 140 Cases of Technology-Facilitated Sexual Violence in 2019, the Most Ever in One Year," December 2, 2020, https://www.aware.org.sg/2020/12/awares-sexual-assault-care-centre-saw-140-cases-of-technology-facilitated-sexual-violence-in-2019-the-most-ever-in-one-year.

The research should include information on:

- Where youths get their sexual information
- What sexual behaviours they are engaging in and at what age
- What challenges they face in their sexual lives, especially in relation to porn, sexting, sexual exploitation
- Youths' values, skills and knowledge on sexual matters
- Youths' views on how school sex education programmes can be improved

It is crucial for the voices of young people to be included in the creation of a sex education programme that meets their needs.

Gender Equality Education in Schools

The consistent feedback from youths is that our current sex education is inadequate. It is too focused on abstinence, risk and disease. Our youths are on the right track. The UN and the World Health Organization (WHO) advocate for countries to provide comprehensive sex education (CSE) that go beyond abstinence-focused sex education.

Instead, CSE should focus on:

... equipping young people with knowledge, skills, attitudes and values that will empower them to:

- *Realise their health, well-being and dignity.*
- *Develop respectful social and sexual relationships.*
- *Consider how their choices affect their own well-being and that of others.*
- *Understand and ensure the protection of their rights throughout their lives.*[35]

---

[35] UNESCO, *International Technical Guidance on Sexuality Education: An Evidence-Informed Approach* (Place de Fontenoy: UNESCO; Geneva: UNAIDS Secretariat; New York: The United Nations Population Fund; New York: The United Children's Fund; New York: UN Women; Geneva: The World Health Organization, 2018), 18.

To assist countries, the UN and WHO jointly issued the *International Technical Guidance on Sexuality Education* in 2018 to help countries develop and implement CSE. The UN guide says that CSE programmes should promote:

> *The right to choose when and with whom a person will have any form of intimate or sexual relationship; the responsibility of these choices; and respecting the choices of others in this regard. This choice includes the right to abstain, to delay, or to engage in sexual relationships.*[36]

In other words, sex education should not focus on just promoting abstinence. The guide recognises that sex education is meant to provide life skills. Abstinence is not a permanent condition in most people's lives. Young people will soon need these skills when they become adults. Of course, it should be age appropriate. What we tell someone at 12 years old is very different from what we tell people who are older.

What else should it include? First, CSE must focus on consent, respect and healthy relationships. Second, it should cover gender norms and stereotypes. Research shows that curricula focused on gender issues and power dynamics are five times more effective at reducing rates of sexually transmitted infections and unintended pregnancy than curricula that ignore gender.[37] Third, it must include peer pressure, bullying, harassment and gender-based violence. Lastly, it must educate on the use of digital sexual communications and the availability of porn.

Our government is reviewing the school's sexuality education as part of the gender equality review. I urge the government to be bold in its review and implement a CSE programme for all schools based on best practices. If we do not get this right, the default educator is porn, which our young boys are already accessing at 13. We are failing our kids if we

---

[36] Ibid.

[37] Nicole A. Haberland, "The Case for Addressing Gender and Power in Sexuality and HIV Education: A Comprehensive Review of Evaluation Studies," *International Perspectives on Sexual and Reproductive Health* 41, no. 1 (2015): 1.

do not provide these critical life skills that they need to navigate this sexualised world.

Parents who are not comfortable with their children going through a more comprehensive programme should be given a chance to opt out. But they should not hold back the education of the next generation of kids. To implement CSE, we must invest in training CSE teachers who are able to adopt an empathetic, sensitive and non-judgmental approach to sex education, who understand youth culture and are gender-informed.

A final note on promoting gender equality in schools. There are lots of opportunities to educate our youths on this. Not just through our Character and Citizenship Education (CCE) or Sex Education programmes. It can be included in literally every subject. Here are some ideas:

- There is a delightful and educational book called *Awesome Women in Singapore*. It is produced by the Singapore Council of Women's Organisations. It is full of stories and illustrations of famous women scientists, activists, artists, entrepreneurs and other outstanding Singaporean women. A book like this can be used by arts, science and history teachers to inspire kids about the women who broke barriers and made history.
- For English, you could facilitate a debate between kids on "Women are the Stronger Sex".
- For CCE, you could conduct a project to interview family members and friends about how they have experienced gender roles and expectations in their lives.

If our teachers are gender-trained, the possibilities for stimulating young minds to learn about gender in the real world are endless. Once they see the inequalities, they will naturally work towards fixing it. So, the starting point is to include gender education in our teachers' training programme.

When teachers get it, the rest will follow. If we are to make gender a fundamental value in Singapore, we need to train our educators about gender and encourage them to build this into their class activities.

Let this be in the government's White Paper on gender equality!

The Future

We are reaching the end of the lecture series. What a journey! From the 1950s till today. What does the future hold for us? More than ever, I am hopeful and excited about the future of gender equality in Singapore. Here is why.

Game Changer #1: Inspired by #MeToo. Women Speaking Up. Changing Systems.

Inspired by #MeToo, women speak up and change systems. #MeToo changed the world, Singapore included. Its ripples of change created further ripples, as women spoke up publicly against their perpetrators and systems that allowed perpetrators to get away too easily.

Here are two cases where public complaints led to major systemic changes. First, Monica Baey's Instagram posts about the mishandling of her voyeurism case caused the National University of Singapore (NUS) to review and revamp its harassment policies and to train its staff and student leaders. The second, national hurdler Kerstin Ong's complaints about Sport Singapore's handling of her case resulted in the national sports agency creating a new framework on managing harassment in sports.

These public cases are just the tip of the iceberg. #MeToo shifted the whole iceberg, for good. And it is still shifting:

- Calls to AWARE's Sexual Assault Care Centre rose sharply after #MeToo. They continue to rise.
- AWARE's monthly Sexual Assault First Responder training sells out within a day. Young people want to know how to support their friends who have been assaulted.
- Companies got the memo. Many have invested in initiatives to create more inclusive and respectful workplaces.
- Men have also told me that they have changed the way they date.

Game Changer #2: Fatherhood. Transforming Masculinity.

I talked about fatherhood in the second lecture and how dads in Singapore are becoming much more active fathers. Fatherhood brings out the gentler and more emotional natures of men. That is why it is so important for equal parenting leave. It not only helps women, but also goes a long way to reduce toxic masculinity.

Let me just share this quote with you by Michael Kaufman, the founder of the White Ribbon Campaign, a global campaign where men take a stand against violence. He said:

> *The transformation of fatherhood will be, for men, what feminism has been for women. It is the thing that is redefining our lives in a powerful, life-affirming, forward-moving way.*[38]

Like many others who started with work to end violence against women, Kaufman sees fatherhood as a very positive way of liberating men from their prisons of masculinity.

Game Changer #3: Gender Equality Review

The government's current gender equality review, with the ambitious and inspiring aim to "imprint gender equality deeply into our collective consciousness", promises to be a game changer.

As I said in my first lecture, the ground is so ripe for this, and the government is doing the right thing, at the right time.

Today, we celebrate the 60th Anniversary of the Women's Charter. This was our first major breakthrough in the women's rights movement of Singapore. I hope that one day, we will look back and celebrate the gender equality review as a historical event — the moment of pivot when Singapore started to embrace gender equality and never looked back.

---

[38] Michael Kaufman, *The Time Has Come: Why Men Must Join the Gender Equality Revolution* (Berkeley: Counterpoint, 2019).

On my part, I have come up with many ideas to take the conversation to the next level and to provide a vision for gender equality in Singapore. I commit to do whatever I can to support the work of the gender equality review.

I promised a toast in my first lecture to celebrate the 60th Anniversary of the Women's Charter. Here's to all of you who care about and continue to work on this issue in your families, schools, workplaces and society. Cheers! To the next 60 years. Let us continue to fight the good fight — for a more caring society, for a gender-equal Singapore.

Question-and-Answer Session
Moderated by Ms Eunice Olsen

Ms Eunice Olsen: Hello everyone, thank you so much for tuning into this. Thank you for all your questions, there has been a lot of engaging discussions going on in our Facebook comments so please keep the conversations going.

Thank you, Corinna, for that insightful lecture; it really brought the three lectures to a close very nicely because you dealt with some deep core issues of gender equality. I'm privileged to be here and to be a part of this conversation. Singapore, at this point in time, is going through a difficult period and so is the rest of the world. But these are really important and necessary conversations to have because at the end of the day, we have to ask ourselves what is the kind of nation that we want to emerge in a post-COVID world.

As much as it takes collective effort to work and overcome the pandemic, it also takes that similar endeavour for gender equality. You have talked so much about the policies that we need to put in place, and you have put forward some very good suggestions today. While we wait for the release of the government's gender equality review later this year, what can men do on an individual level to help move the needle towards gender parity?

Ms Corinna Lim: We can probably take our cues from how women have done this in the past, when women started reflecting on their own situation in small groups and thinking about the unfairness of gender inequality.

For men who want to take action, I think reflection is the first step. To ask the question: What can I do if I care about gender equality? I have heard cases of men, who are fathers, making changes in their workplace because they were inspired to recreate a better place in this world for their daughters. If they are leaders in their workplace, they can start by making sure that their co-workers do not have unconscious gender biases or they are made aware of this by getting training, talking about it and implementing new policies to deal with sexual harassment in the workplace.

It is very difficult for any one person or even a few people to change their behaviour when the rest of the group is making it very difficult for them to speak up, especially with the threat of ostracism and loss of their social capital. The environment has to actually say, "We don't like this kind of behaviour. We want to have respectful workplaces." That is why shifting structures and organisations will help. We cannot expect this work to be done just by individuals.

Let us take the men's WhatsApp group chats, for example. I have been thinking about what men could do when they are in a private group situation. If there is one man there who is feeling uncomfortable about the conversations, there are probably others feeling the same way too, except no one is saying anything.

So, he could have side conversations with someone else in the group to express his discomfort on what was just circulated, without exposing himself to the whole group. This will also allow him to conduct a sensing of the group to see if others are feeling the same way. You can probably take action, such as exiting the group once you achieve critical mass — usually around 30 per cent. Alternatively, if you feel that this group might be helpful to you and leaving may not be such a good idea, you could speak privately with the person who is sending the message without calling him out or making him "lose face" in the group.

Regarding the family situation: The Asian family seems to be quite a cold and unaffectionate unit. You may not even see the husband and wife holding hands, which is not good for the children. Boys need to see men comfortable with their feelings and emotionally connecting with women. It's not just about being affectionate with your kids, but about being a loving person and not being afraid to show that. For example, my dad was aloof and cold because he was uncomfortable with his emotions. It was awkward until his last 10 years when all of that dissolved. If men could just take these small steps with their own family, it might go some ways.

Ms Olsen: Absolutely. You would want to show, especially your children, that it is perfectly all right to have affections and express your emotions, whether positive or negative.

Ms Lim: Boys learn that their first role model in life is their father. However, many of the men I interviewed had fathers who were very distant. They were either working very hard and sometimes not even in the same country or were emotionally absent because similarly, they also had fathers who were distant. Many men who have had emotionally distant dads become distant with their own children as well. Thus, there is a need to understand that your son is observing you closely. That your behaviour may be feeding his brains with this image that fathers are supposed to be emotionally disciplined and distant. I think fathers ought to re-examine this and put themselves in the shoes of their children. How do you think they are seeing you as a person and how you treat your wives and kids?

Ms Olsen: I want to get to our viewers' questions. The issue on NS has been quite a hot topic on Facebook. What is your opinion on women who go through childbirth, do housework and take care of families, wouldn't asking them to do NS pose as an additional burden for them? We have had quite a few responses to that.

Ms Lim: NS is one of those things that we need to talk about. I am not too sure exactly what the final solution is. Asking a woman who is already a mother to do NS is a bit too much. I think that NS will be more suitable for younger women who are not yet mothers. I do not think that it is too much to ask for. If men can do it, I would say that women can too. I do not want to think of giving birth as NS. In my view, that is not the right idea.

Right now, the problem about women giving birth is childcare. It should be both parties and not just the woman's role. We should be socialising the idea that both men and women can do NS, are equal parents and have equal responsibilities. They can choose to divide up the roles the way they want but both men and women are equally responsible for domestic care and the caregiving of the child. So, I can understand why people feel that women's participation in NS is asking a lot from women, but only because women still do twice the amount of housework and caregiving in the family today.

Ms Olsen: Going back to the idea of patriarchy versus matriarchy, we have a question that says, "Why would men work towards creating a patriarchy that works against men?" Furthermore, doesn't a matriarchy, for example, some Peranakan households, tend to regress into tyrannical hierarchies as well?

Ms Lim: I am not too familiar with the Peranakan households. Nonetheless, when you look at the lives of men in the stories I shared during the lecture, they are not allowed to connect to their own feelings and I think that is such a huge cost to pay as a human being. I think about my dad's life — which is why it saddens me so much — and how as a young person, I did not know how to reach out to him. Even as an older person, I feel that he did most of the reaching out in the last 10 years because I was just kind of stiff. It is such a huge cost to pay for men to benefit from the patriarchy. I think men have to choose if they want to continue living in such a way. Look at all the downsides of it — the crime rates, alcohol and drug abuse. We have never thought of this as a men's problem, but in reality, it is. We do not see the same number of women with these issues than we do with men.

So, if we start to really think about it, I think that men might see that they have a lot to lose in a patriarchy.

Ms Olsen: I think there was a comment that said that taking down the patriarchy does not mean replacing it with a matriarchy. We are talking about creating a gender-equal world. At the end of the day, we are looking at how men have a role to play in the entire gender conversation.

Ms Lim: Yes, the idea here is that no one should be restricted to their roles. Usually, we think of girls and their dads encouraging them to be anything they want to be when they grow up. Unfortunately, boys do not have that same freedom. It is more restrictive for them due to the policing of behaviour with masculine norms. I asked AWARE to put out a question, "In today's age, would you prefer to be a man or a woman?" Interestingly, the response was 50:50. Aside from NS obligations, some women preferred to be a man, citing greater privileges. However, many people said they wanted to be able to feel, cry and be more emotionally expressive.

Ms Olsen: Actually, it is good that some men recognise and acknowledge that being a man comes with privileges. On the topic of toxic masculinity, do women have a part in contributing to toxic masculinity too? Some women say that they are sexually attracted to men who are more masculine in their behaviour. How can the society shift to allow men to be whoever they are?

Ms Lim: For sure, women are also part of the problem. In fact, it is not about men or women. It is about patriarchal norms in society, which are nested in our heads and in every social interaction that we have with a man or woman. Women who tease men about being too effeminate are part of the problem and that is going to make this change difficult. So, we need to have this conversation and it starts with personal reflection. There is a feminist mantra that I really like: "The personal is political." Start looking at your personal biases and situation if you want to make change. We all have a part to play and women are definitely part of this problem.

Ms Olsen: This goes back to your earlier point. As much as it is hard sometimes for individuals to call out or do something, self-reflection is crucial before the bigger structures of change can be put in place.

Ms Lim: The personal is political. We need to bear in mind that, even as personal agency is important, people make personal decisions within an existing social and policy framework. So, it is also important to look at the existing structures, such as the values embedded in NS, family leave, our education system, to see how it shapes personal values and decisions. To inculcate a gender equal mindset, we should start by training our teachers about gender equality and how to promote this in our education system. This will then trickle down to their students. Children understand fairness instinctively. They recognise injustice when they see it. It will not be too difficult for adults to affirm children's instincts about why girls and boys should have equal opportunities and encourage them to call out injustices when they see it.

Ms Olsen: I have a question on sexuality education, since you have talked a little bit about teachers. We often hear the statement: If you talk about it, you are encouraging it. With regard to sexuality education and how some believe it will encourage children to engage in sexual activity, what are your thoughts?

Ms Lim: The United Nations' (UN) *International Technical Guidance on Sexuality Education* in 2018 that I spoke about during my lecture did a massive review of all of the evidence, it came to a very clear conclusion that CSE delays first-time sex among youths and results in younger people having fewer sexual partners and practising more safe sex habits. In fact, promoting sexuality education protects the well-being of our children as it reduces the likelihood of adolescents engaging in sexual activities at an earlier age. This has been our experience as sex education trainers in international schools. We did surveys before and after sex education and found that many youths came to the conclusion on their own accord that they were just not ready for sex. It is impressive that they are able to make this decision with the relevant considerations when empowered to think for themselves.

Ms Olsen: I have a question here about the #MeToo movement. The #MeToo movement has been a net positive that is encouraging women to speak out and report sexual harassment. However, it seems to promote a "trial by social media" without any due process that establishes their guilt, perpetuating a "guilty until proven innocent" culture. What are your thoughts on this? Is there any way we can mitigate this without undermining the good that the #MeToo movement has done?

Ms Lim: This is a tough one because social media is a way for people without power to call offenders out. That is the good thing. But there is a negative side to it, which I don't really know what to do about. I did think in the course of preparing these lectures that Singapore might do well with an apology law. I have come across many instances, not just on social media but with other sexual harassment cases, where the perpetrator knows that he or she did something wrong but is unable to apologise, as they might be admitting liability.

An apology law allows people to give their apology without legal liability. It may or may not be accepted by the other party, but at least he or she has a chance to do so should they really feel remorseful without the admission of guilt in a court of law. There has to be more ways that we can deal with these offences than just social media. Our criminal justice system is harsh and there are not a lot of opportunities for rehabilitation. Perhaps we can build more ways for mediation in the criminal justice system. For example, if someone brings a complaint, then the police could suggest arranging for a mediated settlement. We also want the offender to receive treatment, which is not available in the current system. For instance, the Mandatory Treatment Order is not usually used in these sexual harassment cases. There must be a more diverse range of ways that we can deal with these offences.

The attacks and smears on social media are quite difficult to contain. I do not know if I see it as promoting a "guilty until proven innocent" culture. But I see that everyone is getting upset and we are not getting any closer to a solution. The person who is making the complaint is also very victimised by the divisiveness and polarisation on social media.

Ms Olsen: Because as much as you may receive support, you might also get vitriol.

Ms Lim: Yes, it is highly upsetting. So, I sometimes think it's a lose–lose situation. In that sense, it is very unsatisfactory.

Ms Olsen: Just going back to something that you said before about the feminist lens. If you have that feminist lens, whether it is on policy or even the criminal justice system, it will change the perspective of what you put forward and we can think about building that into our systems.

Ms Lim: Where there are organisations involved, it is a bit better. The hard ones are where you are calling someone out and it is not in a workplace situation. In organisations, there is at least a person in charge of dealing with such conflicts. But for social media, it is a free-for-all, where everyone is in the community and the platform is the only way to call out the offender.

Ms Olsen: It is one way to say that the assault happened and seek help. To speak up and reach out.

Ms Lim: I also think that people are not sufficiently well informed about what constitutes sexual assault and harassment. For instance, I might feel that someone has done something to disrespect me but the other person does not get it, which then devolves into an argument at different levels. So long as that person has reasonably felt hurt, then that is a problem, and it is harassment. It is not about intention and many people did not get that for a long time. If you do not understand this concept, you will feel aggrieved that someone has accused you and would say, "I didn't intend to hurt you." I think public education in general would be extremely helpful here.

Ms Olsen: Moving on to this question on penalties for sex crimes. The government recently raised penalties for sex crimes this year. Do you think this is sufficient? Should more be done to punish and deter sexual offenders?

Ms Lim: The punishment has to be adequate. Making it unnecessarily harsh has definite downsides. In our experience in this line of work, many survivors want some accountability but not necessarily for the person to be punished so harshly — it might deter people from reporting the offence. What is more important is that when you report, the case is taken up. This reporting and investigation process is more important than the punishment itself. If potential perpetrators know the criminal system is efficient and there is a high chance that they will be taken to task, then it will serve as deterrence. It is not so much the punishment but rather the public shaming that is the biggest deterrence for many cases.

I think the recent changes were great because they made voyeurism and upskirting very specific crimes. It is more about the system — that when you go to the police, they will take up the case. And the police have been improving the way that they deal with these cases too.

Ms Olsen: I think a lot of them also say that they don't want this to happen to someone else, which comes up a lot when people report.

Ms Lim: That is why we always say if that is the case, just report. The act of the police calling up someone can be a very good deterrent, even if the police decide not to proceed with the case. Still, the system can be a lot gentler with the victim. I find that the whole criminal justice system is a tough system to go through. There are things that I feel can still be tweaked to improve the victim's experience through the system. They have done a lot of improvements at the court level but just even having to wait one year at least, where you have to keep telling the story before you have your day in court, is potentially traumatic for the victim. We have asked for a specialised court so that these cases are fast-tracked and the officials there are gender and trauma-informed, to ensure a smooth process in the system from beginning to end.

Ms Olsen: In your case study of a boy victim of sexual harassment, you discussed how masculine norms caused him not to report the harassment. Do you think there are other major factors apart from masculine norms that are preventing male victims to speak up?

Ms Lim: I think that for both men and women, it's hard to complain about sexual harassment. There is a lot of stigma and differentiated norms unique to both men and women that prevent them from reporting the assault. For Tim, he was not told or aware about sexual assault. I don't think that men and boys get the same kind of advice on seeking help as girls do, in relation to sexual assault. So, one — men don't get as much attention in this area. Two — as a male, you are supposed to just "suck it up", "be a man", and present yourself in a heterosexual way. For women, there are a lot of norms involved that we have been talking about. For instance, victim blaming is still rampant.

I chose to focus this lecture on men even though there are a lot of issues that women face. I specifically wanted to highlight masculine norms because this impacts women at the end of the day. To stop sexual assault, we have to work with both men and women. Of course, we will continue to support women through all of the stigmas that they are facing. That work has to go on. But someone needs to work on the men — not AWARE — but we can support others to do it.

Ms Olsen: I'm hoping after this lecture a group of people will step up to do this.

Ms Lim: Me too. And hopefully with a more feminist lens.

Ms Olsen: I have a question on leadership. Do you have a message for leadership in government, educational institutions and corporate organisations to move our society towards gender parity?

Ms Lim: I tried to use these lectures to provide some education on gender — why men and women behave differently, their different lived experiences and how supportive environments can bring out the best in both men and women. If we have that focus of what we can do to bring out the best in men and women while understanding the gender experience they live through, I think that would be the way forward. So, I hope that gender education becomes a part of our school curriculum. For adults, I hope that you can learn more and engage in conversations by immersing yourself in these topics.

Ms Olsen: Corinna, it's been a huge privilege having this conversation with you and I want to thank you for all the hard work that you've done, together with the people who have helped you put together these amazing lectures — the first ever on gender equality. I seriously hope that the government will take your points into consideration for our upcoming gender review, which I am sure all of us are very much looking forward to.

Ms Lim: Thank you. The gender equality review is such a massive opportunity for us to say what we want in relation to gender equality and how we should move forward. There are many ways that you can make your ideas, wishes and views known. There are conversations going on, both organised by the government and AWARE, where you can write in to contribute. It is not going to go on forever, so please, this is the right time to get involved.

If you like this lecture series, please share it with as many people as possible. I've tried to push the envelope a little bit further and some of these ideas are on the wilder side. Maybe these changes will not happen today, but it is important to plant that seed. Who knows, in 10 years' time, it might happen.

Bibliography

Abdullah, Zhaki. "Singapore to Embark on a Review of Women's Issues in Move Towards Greater Gender Equality, Leading to White Paper Next Year." *CNA*, September 20, 2020. https://www.channelnewsasia.com/news/singapore/gender-equality-womens-issues-singapore-to-embark-engagements--13126778.

American Psychological Association, Boys and Men Guidelines Group. "APA Guidelines for Psychological Practice with Boys and Men." August 2018. https://www.apa.org/about/policy/boys-men-practice-guidelines.pdf.

Amodia-Bidakowska, Annabel, Ciara Laverty, and Paul G. Ramchandani. "Father-Child Play: A Systematic Review of its Frequency, Characteristics and Potential Impact on Children's Development." *Developmental Review* 57, no. 100924 (2020): 1–17.

Arehart-Treichel, Joan. "Childhood Bullying Correlates with Adult Domestic Violence." *Psychiatric News* 47, no. 1 (2012): 12–16.

Astone, Nan Marie, and H. Elizabeth Peters. "Longitudinal Influences on Men's Lives: Research from the Transition to Fatherhood Project and Beyond." *Fathering* 12, no. 2 (Spring 2014): 161–73.

Awang, Nabilah, and Tessa Oh. "Let's Talk About Safe Sex: Sex Education Should Go Beyond Preaching Abstinence, Say Students and Experts." *Today*, October 28, 2019. https://www.todayonline.com/singapore/lets-talk-about-safe-sex-sex-education-should-go-beyond-preaching-abstinence-say-students.

Association of Women for Action and Research (AWARE). "AWARE's Sexual Assault Care Centre Saw 140 Cases of Technology-Facilitated Sexual Violence in 2019, the Most Ever in One Year." December 2, 2020. https://www.aware.org.sg/2020/12/awares-sexual-assault-care-centre-saw-140-cases-of-technology-facilitated-sexual-violence-in-2019-the-most-ever-in-one-year.

———. "Make Care Count: The Impact of Eldercare on the Retirement Adequacy of Female Caregivers." September 2019. https://www.aware.org.sg/wp-content/uploads/Aware_Eldercare-Research-Report-8-10-19.pdf.

———. "Only Half of Parents Are Comfortable Talking to Their Kids About Sex Ed, While Most Prefer School Programmes to Focus on Consent Over Abstinence: AWARE-Blackbox Survey." July 1, 2020. https://www.aware.org.sg/2020/07/parents-comfortable-sex-ed-consent-abstinence-aware-blackbox-survey.

———. "Remaking Singapore: Views of Half the Nation." 2002. https://www.aware. org.sg/wp-content/uploads/Remaking_Singapore.pdf.

———. "'Why Are You Not Working?': Low-Income Mothers Explain Challenges with Work & Care." 2018. https://d2t1lspzrjtif2.cloudfront.net/wp-content/ uploads/Advocacy-report-why-are-you-not-working-updated-2-April-2019. pdf.

AWARE, and the Humanitarian Organization for Migration Economics (HOME). "Neither Family Nor Employee: The Caregiver Burden of Migrant Domestic Workers in Singapore." November 2020. https://www.aware.org.sg/wp-content/ uploads/Neither-Family-Nor-Employee-AWARE-HOME-Report-Nov-2020.pdf.

Barker, Gary, Juan Manuel Contreras, Brian Heilman, Ajay Singh, and Marcos Nascimento. "Evolving Men: Initial Results from the International Men and Gender Equality Survey (IMAGES)." *International Center for Research on Women* and *Instituto Promundo*, June 2011. https://promundoglobal.org/wp-content/uploads/2014/12/Evolving-Men-Initial-Results-from-IMAGES.pdf.

Bartlett, Edward E. "The Effects of Fatherhood on the Health of Men: A Review of the Literature." *The Journal of Men's Health & Gender* 1, no. 2–3 (2004): 159–69.

Brown, Jane D., and Kelly L. L'Engle. "X-Rated: Sexual Attitudes and Behaviors Associated with U.S. Early Adolescents' Exposure to Sexually Explicit Media." *Communication Research* 36, no. 1 (2009): 129–51.

Burgess, Adrienne. "The Costs and Benefits of Active Fatherhood: Evidence and Insights to Inform the Development of Policy and Practice." *Fathers Direct*, 2008. https://www.fatherhood.gov/research-and-resources/costs-and-benefits-active-fatherhood-evidence-and-insights-inform-development.

Carmody, Moira, Michael Salter, and Geir Henning Presterudstuen. *Less to Lose and More to Gain? Men and Boys Violence Prevention Research Project: Final Report.* Australia: University of Western Sydney, 2014.

Chan, Choy Siong. Speech given to the First Parliament on the Women's Charter Bill. April 6, 1960. *Hansard Parliamentary Debates* 12 (1960).

Chan, Heng Chee. *World in Transition: Singapore's Future.* Singapore: World Scientific, 2021.

Cheow, Sue-Ann. "Men Twice as Likely to Commit Suicide." *The New Paper*, April 29, 2019. https://www.tnp.sg/news/singapore/men-twice-likely-commit-suicide.

Chew, Hui Min. "Singapore's Total Fertility Rate Falls to Historic Low in 2020." *CNA*, February 25, 2021. https://www.channelnewsasia.com/news/singapore/singapore-total-fertility-rate-tfr-falls-historic-low-2020-baby-14288556.

Chew, Melanie. *Leaders of Singapore*. Singapore: Resource Press, 1996.

Chew, Phyllis Ghim-Lian. "The Singapore Council of Women and the Women's Movement." *Journal of Southeast Asian Studies* 25, no. 1 (1994): 112–40.

Chew, Phyllis Ghim-Lian, Jenny Lin Lam, Singapore Council of Women's Organisations, and Singapore Baha'i Women's Committee. *Voices & Choices: The Women's Movement in Singapore*. Singapore: Singapore Council of Women's Organisations and Singapore Baha'i Women's Committee, 1993.

Chua, Mui Hoong, and Rachel Chang. "Did Mr Lee Kuan Yew Create a Singapore in His Own Image?" *The Straits Times*, March 24, 2015. https://www.straitstimes.com/singapore/did-mr-lee-kuan-yew-create-a-singapore-in-his-own-image.

Chua, Seng Chew, and Singapore Department of Statistics. *State of Singapore, Report on the Census of Population: 1957*. Singapore: Lim Bian Han, Government Printer, 1964.

Cislaghi, Beniamino, and Lori Heise. "Gender Norms and Social Norms: Differences, Similarities and Why they Matter in Prevention Science." *Sociology of Health & Illness* 42, no. 2 (2020): 407–22.

Connolly, Jennifer, Debra Pepler, Wendy Craig, and Ali Taradash. "Dating Experiences of Bullies in Early Adolescence." *Child Maltreatment* 5, no. 4 (2000): 299–310.

Dines, Gail, Robert Jensen, and Ann Russo. *Pornography: The Production and Consumption of Inequality*. New York: Routledge, 1998.

Espelage, Dorothy L., Kathleen C. Basile, and Merle E. Hamburger. "Bullying Perpetration and Subsequent Sexual Violence Perpetration among Middle School Students." *Journal of Adolescent Health* 50, no. 1 (2012): 60–65.

Espelage, Dorothy L., Kathleen C. Basile, Lisa De La Rue, and Merle E. Hamburger. "Longitudinal Associations Among Bullying, Homophobic Teasing, and Sexual Violence Perpetration Among Middle School Students." *Journal of Interpersonal Violence* 30, no. 14 (2015): 2541–61.

Espelage, Dorothy L., Kathleen C. Basile, Ruth W. Leemis, Tracy N. Hipp, and Jordan P. Davis. "Longitudinal Examination of the Bullying-Sexual Violence Pathway Across Early to Late Adolescence: Implicating Homophobic Name-Calling." *Journal of Youth and Adolescence* 47, no. 9 (2018): 1880–93.

Espelage, Dorothy L., Sabina Low, Carolyn Anderson, and Lisa De La Rue. "Relation Between Bully & Teen Dating Violence Perpetration Across Early to Late Adolescence." Press release, August 2018. https://www.apa.org/news/press/releases/2013/08/bully-dating.pdf.

Frost, Mark Ravinder, and Yu-Mei Balasingamchow. *Singapore: A Biography.* Singapore: Editions Didier Millet, 2012.

Gan, Yunn Hwen, and Sophia Archuleta. "Holding Up Half the Sky — Women in Singapore Medicine." *Singapore Medical Association* 52, no. 2 (February 2020): 20–23.

Gilmore, Jane. "We Know Violence, Crime and Masculinity Are Linked. It's Time to Look at Why, and How to Stop It." *The Sydney Morning Herald*, October 19, 2017. https://www.smh.com.au/lifestyle/we-know-violence-crime-and-masculinity-are-linked-its-time-to-look-at-why-and-how-to-stop-it-20171019-gz3zq3.html.

Goldman, Rebecca, and National Family and Parenting Institute. *Fathers' Involvement in Their Children's Education: A Review of Research and Practice.* London: National Family and Parenting Institute, 2005.

Government of Canada. "Backgrounder — The Government of Canada Invests in Engaging Men and Boys in Gender Equality," November 26, 2020. https://www.canada.ca/en/women-gender-equality/news/2019/08/backgrounder--the-government-of-canada-invests-in-engaging-men-and-boys-in-gender-equality.html.

"Government's Hard-Nosed Approach Defended." *The Straits Times*, April 20, 1987, 15.

Goy, Priscilla. "Big Increase in Childcare Places, MOE Kindergartens." *The Straits Times*, August 21, 2017. https://www.straitstimes.com/singapore/big-increase-in-childcare-places-moe-kindergartens.

Haberland, Nicole A. "The Case for Addressing Gender and Power in Sexuality and HIV Education: A Comprehensive Review of Evaluation Studies." *International Perspectives on Sexual and Reproductive Health* 41, no. 1 (2015): 31–42.

Herrero, Juan, Andrea Torres, Francisco J. Rodríguez, and Joel Juarros-Basterretxea. "Intimate Partner Violence Against Women in the European Union: The Influence of Male Partners' Traditional Gender Roles and General Violence." *Psychology of Violence* 7, no. 3 (2017): 385–94.

Ho, Elaine L. E., Shirlene Huang, and Lien Foundation. *Care Where You Are.* Singapore: Straits Times Press, 2018.

Ho, Kwon Ping. *The Ocean in a Drop: Singapore: The Next Fifty Years.* Singapore: World Scientific, 2015.

Ho, Peter. *The Challenges of Governance in a Complex World.* Singapore: World Scientific, 2017.

Jeynes, William H. "A Meta-Analysis: The Relationship Between Father Involvement and Student Academic Achievement." *Urban Education* 50, no. 4 (2015): 387–423.

Kaufman, Michael. *The Time Has Come: Why Men Must Join the Gender Equality Revolution.* Berkeley: Counterpoint, 2019.

Kho, Ee Moi. "Economic Pragmatism and the 'Schooling' of Girls in Singapore." *HSSE Online* 4, no. 2 (October 2015): 62–77.

Kim, Erin Hye-Won. "Division of Domestic Labour and Lowest-Low Fertility in South Korea." *Demographic Research* 37, no. 24 (July–December 2017): 743–68.

Kotila, Letitia E., and Claire M. Kamp Dush. "Involvement with Children and Low-Income Fathers' Psychological Well-being." *Fathering* 11, no. 3 (Fall 2013): 306–26.

Lash, Steven J., Michael M. Copenhaver, and Richard M. Eisler. "Masculine Gender Role Stress and Substance Abuse Among Substance Dependent Males." *Journal of Gender, Culture, and Health* 3, no. 3 (1998): 183–91.

Lee, Kuan Yew. "National Day Rally Speech 1986." Speech given at National Day Rally, Singapore, 1986.

———. *The Singapore Story: Memoirs of Lee Kuan Yew.* Singapore: Singapore Press Holdings, 1998.

Levant, Ronald. "Moving Beyond Toxic Masculinity: A Q&A with Ronald Levant." *Oxford University Press Blog*, May 30, 2020. https://blog.oup.com/2020/05/moving-beyond-toxic-masculinity-a-qa-with-ronald-levant.

Lipponen, Lasse, Lynn Ang, Sirene Lim, Jaakko Hilppö, Hongda Lin, Antti Rajala, and Lien Foundation. *Vital Voices for Vital Years 2.* Singapore: Lien Foundation, 2019.

Locke, Benjamin D., and James R. Mahalik. "Examining Masculinity Norms, Problem Drinking, and Athletic Involvement as Predictors of Sexual Aggression in College Men." *Journal of Counseling Psychology* 52, no. 3 (2005): 279–83.

Lowe, John. "Masculinizing National Service: The Cultural Reproduction of Masculinities and Militarization of Male Citizenship in Singapore." *Journal of Gender Studies* 28, no. 6 (2019): 687–98.

Marçal, Katrine. *Who Cooked Adam Smith's Dinner? A Story about Women and Economics.* London: Portobello Books, 2015.

Marshall, Riley L., Colin R. Harbke, and Lisabeth Fisher DiLalla. "The Role of Remembered Parenting on Adult Self-Esteem: A Monozygotic Twin Difference Study." *Behavior Genetics* 51, no. 2 (2021): 125–36.

Ministry of Education. "Sexuality Education: Roles of Stakeholders." Accessed May 20, 2021. https://www.moe.gov.sg/programmes/sexuality-education/stakeholders.

———. "Sexuality Education: Scope and Teaching Approach." Accessed May 20, 2021. https://www.moe.gov.sg/programmes/sexuality-education/scope-and-teaching-approach.

Ministry of Home Affairs. "Conversations on Women Development — Speech by K Shanmugam, Minister for Home Affairs and Minister for Law." September 20, 2020. https://www.mha.gov.sg/mediaroom/speeches/conversations-on-women-development-speech-by-mr-k-shanmugam-minister-for-home-affairs-and-minister-for-law.

Ministry of Home Affairs, Central Narcotics Bureau. "Demographic Profile of Drug Abusers." Accessed May 20, 2021. https://data.gov.sg/dataset/demographic-profile-of-drug-abusers?resource_id=81181cb9-71e4-4a01-b4e2-26.

Ministry of Home Affairs, Singapore Prison Service. "Convicted Penal Population." Accessed May 20, 2021. https://data.gov.sg/dataset/convicted-penal-inmates-population?view_id=c8ab3504-6e16-4314-8c91-2b7298154c84&resource_id=7070dc26-a95a-4560-8670-6682705a9cff.

Ministry of Manpower, Manpower Research and Statistics Department. "Labour Force." [2020 data]. Accessed April 28, 2021. https://stats.mom.gov.sg/Pages/LabourForceTimeSeries.aspx.

———. "Report: Labour Force in Singapore: 2020 Edition." January 28, 2021. https://stats.mom.gov.sg/iMAS_PdfLibrary/mrsd_2020LabourfForce.pdf.

———. "Resident Labour Force Participation Rate by Age and Sex." [2020 data]. Accessed April 4, 2021. https://stats.mom.gov.sg/Pages/LabourForceTimeSeries.aspx.

National Population and Talent Division, Singapore Department of Statistics, Ministry of Home Affairs, Immigration & Checkpoints Authority, and Ministry of Manpower. "Population in Brief 2020." September 2020. https://www.strategygroup.gov.sg/files/media-centre/publications/population-in-brief-2020.pdf.

Ng, Ashton Jing Kai. "Not Justified to Use NS to Teach Women Graciousness." *Today*, November 14, 2019. https://www.todayonline.com/voices/not-justified-use-ns-teach-women-graciousness.

Ng, Desmond. "When Carers Are Burnt Out, Who Cares For Them?" *CNA*, May 5, 2019. https://www.channelnewsasia.com/news/cnainsider/when-carers-caregivers-burnout-who-cares-them-ageing-elderly-11504380.

Ng, Kelly. "S'pore Women More Likely to Suffer From Depression Than Men: IMH Study." *Today*, December 4, 2017. https://www.todayonline.com/singapore/spore-women-more-likely-suffer-depression-men-imh-study.

Organisation for Economic Co-Operation and Development (OECD). "Labour Force Statistics by Sex and Age." Accessed April 4, 2021. https://stats.oecd.org/Index.aspx?DataSetCode=lfs_sexage_i_r.

———. "Fertility Rates." Accessed April 4, 2021. https://data.oecd.org/pop/fertility-rates.htm.

———. "Good for Business: Age Diversity in the Workplace and Productivity." In *Promoting an Age-Inclusive Workforce: Living, Learning and Earning Longer*, 53–79. Paris: OECD Publishing, 2020.

Parent, Mike C., and Bonnie Moradi. "Confirmatory Factor Analysis of the Conformity to Masculine Norms Inventory and Development of the Conformity to Masculine Norms Inventory-46." *Psychology of Men & Masculinity* 10, no. 3 (2009): 175–89.

People's Action Party (PAP). "Women in the New Singapore." In *The Tasks Ahead Part 2: PAP's Five-Year Plan, 1959–1964*, 17–24. Singapore: Petir, 1959.

Prime Minister's Office, Strategy Group, National Population and Talent Division. "2016 Marriage and Parenthood Survey." https://www.population.gov.sg/our-population/population-trends/marriage-&-parenthood.

———. "DPM Teo Chee Hean's Speech on Population at the 2012 Committee of Supply." March 1, 2012. https://www.population.gov.sg/media-centre/speeches/speech-by-dpm-teo-chee-hean-on-population.

———. "Speech by Senior Minister of State Josephine Teo on Population at the Committee of Supply." March 2, 2017. https://www.population.gov.sg/mediacentre/speeches/speech-by-senior-minister-of-state-josephine-teo-onpopulation.

Prime Minister's Office, Strategy Group. "Press Release: Enhanced Marriage & Parenthood Package in Support of a Profamily Environment in Singapore." https://www.strategygroup.gov.sg/images/Press%20Release%20images/PDFs/enhanced-marriage-parenthood-package-in-support-of-a-profamily-environment-in-singapore.pdf.

———. "Speech by DPM Teo Chee Hean on Population White Paper at the Parliamentary Debate." February 4, 2013. https://www.strategygroup.gov.sg/mediacentre/speeches/speech-by-dpm-teo-chee-hean-on-population-white-paper.

Reaching Everyone for Active Citizenry@Home (REACH). "Conversations on Singapore Women's Development." Accessed May 20, 2021. https://www.reach.gov.sg/en/Participate/conversations-on-singapore-womens-development.

Rippon, Gina. *The Gendered Brain: The New Neuroscience that Shatters the Myth of the Female Brain*. London: The Bodley Head, 2019.

Samuels, Michelle. "Porn Isn't There to Teach You What You Are Supposed to Do When You Are Having Sex." *Boston University School of Public Health*, January 6, 2021. https://www.bu.edu/sph/news/articles/2021/young-adults-say-pornography-main-source-of-info.

Santana, M. Christina, Anita Raj, Michele R. Decker, Ana La Marche, and Jay G. Silverman. "Masculine Gender Roles Associated with Increased Sexual Risk and Intimate Partner Violence Perpetration Among Young Adult Men." *Journal of Urban Health* 83, no. 4 (2006): 575–85.

Seah, Kelvin. "Tuition Has Ballooned to a S$1.4b Industry in Singapore: Should We Be Concerned?" *Today*, September 12, 2019. https://www.todayonline.com/commentary/tuition-has-ballooned-s14b-industry-singapore-should-we-be-concerned.

SimilarWeb. "Top Websites Ranking in Singapore." Accessed May 20, 2021. https://www.similarweb.com/top-websites/singapore.

Sin, Yuen. "Singapore Has Third Highest Rate of Bullying Globally: Study." *The Straits Times*, August 20, 2017. https://www.straitstimes.com/singapore/education/republic-has-third-highest-rate-of-bullying-globally.

Singapore Department of Statistics. "Education, Language Spoken and Literacy." [2019 data]. Accessed May 18, 2021. https://www.singstat.gov.sg/find-data/search-by-theme/population/education-language-spoken-and-literacy/latest-data.

———. "Labour, Employment, Wages and Productivity." [2020 data]. Accessed April 28, 2021. https://www.tablebuilder.singstat.gov.sg/publicfacing/createDataTable.action? refId=12374.

———. "Resident Total Fertility Rate." [1980–2020 data]. Accessed April 4, 2021. https://www.singstat.gov.sg/modules/infographics/total-fertility-rate.

"Speech by the Prime Minister, Mr Lee Kuan Yew, at the NTUC's International Women's Year Seminar cum Exhibition at the DBS Auditorium on Monday, 1 September, 1975." National Archives of Singapore. Accessed May 18, 2021. https://www.nas.gov.sg/archivesonline/data/pdfdoc/lky19750901.pdf.

Tai, Janice. "Nine in 10 Teen Boys in Singapore Exposed to Porn: Survey." *The Straits Times*, June 29, 2016. https://www.straitstimes.com/singapore/nine-in-10-teen-boys-exposed-to-porn-survey.

Teng, Amelia. "Women Take on More Childcare, Even When in Full-Time Work: Poll." *The Straits Times*, June 22, 2020. https://www.straitstimes.com/singapore/women-take-on-more-childcare-even-when-in-full-time-work-poll.

Teo, Anna. "It's Been an Honour, Mr Lee." *Business Times,* March 24, 2015. https://www.businesstimes.com.sg/government-economy/lee-kuan-yew-dies/its-been-an-honour-mr-lee.

Teo, You Yenn. "'Be Decent Mother, Go Through PSLE': When Children's Education Becomes Parental Care Labour." *Academia SG*, February 24, 2021. https://www.academia.sg/academic-views/be-decent-mother-go-through-psle-when-childrens-education-becomes-parental-care-labor.

Thomas, Margaret. "Goodbye to Those Days, When Women of Were 'Pieces of Meat for Men to Slice.'" *CNA*, March 31, 2021. https://www.channelnewsasia.com/news/commentary/womens-rights-singapore-issues-history-parliament-gender-equalit-13230626.

United Nations Children's Fund (UNICEF). "Gender Equality." Accessed May 10, 2021. https://www.unicef.org/gender-equality.

United Nations Committee on the Elimination of Discrimination against Women (CEDAW). "General Recommendation No. 25, on Article 4, Paragraph 1, of the Convention on the Elimination of All Forms of Discrimination Against Women, on Temporary Special Measures." Thirtieth Session, 2004. Accessed June 6, 2021. https://www.un.org/womenwatch/daw/cedaw/recommendations/General%20recommendation%2025%20(English).pdf.

United Nations Economic and Social Commission for Asia and the Pacific (ESCAP). "Long-Term Care of Older Persons in Singapore." June 15, 2016. https://www.unescap.org/sites/default/d8files/Theme-Study-References.pdf.

United Nations Educational, Scientific and Cultural Organization (UNESCO). *International Technical Guidance on Sexuality Education: An Evidence-Informed Approach.* Place de Fontenoy: UNESCO; Geneva: UNAIDS Secretariat; New York: The United Nations Population Fund; New York: The United Children's Fund; New York: UN Women; Geneva: The World Health Organization, 2018.

United Nations Entity for Gender Equality and the Empowerment of Women (UN Women). "Concepts and Definitions." Accessed May 10, 2021. https://www.un.org/womenwatch/osagi/conceptsandefinitions.htm.

Vandello, Joseph A., Jennifer K. Bosson, Dov Cohen, Rochelle M. Burnaford, and Jonathan R. Weaver. "Precarious Manhood." *Journal of Personal Social Psychology* 95, no. 6 (December 2008): 1325–39.

Vaswani, Anmol. "Is There a Need for Better Sex Education That's More Than STDs and Abstinence?" *Millennials of SG*, August 19, 2018. https://mosg.tv/2018/08/19/is-there-a-need-for-better-sex-education-thats-more-than-stds-and-abstinence.

Vera-Gray, Fiona, Clare McGlynn, Ibad Kureshi, and Kate Butterby. "Sexual Violence as a Sexual Script in Mainstream Online Pornography." *The British Journal of Criminology* 61, no. 3 (2021): 1–18.

Wee, Shiou-Liang, Chang Liu, Soon-Noi Goh, Wayne F. Chong, Amudha Aravindhan, and Angelique Chan. "Determinants of Use of Community-Based Long-Term Care Services." *Journal of the American Geriatrics Society (JAGS)* 62, no. 9 (2014): 1801–3.

White Ribbon Campaign. "Give Love, Get Love. The Involved Fatherhood and Gender Equity Project." January 2014. https://www.whiteribbon.ca/uploads/1/1/3/2/113222347/fatherhood_report.pdf.

"Why Intake of Women Into Medical Faculty Cut: Toh." *The Straits Times*, March 17, 1979, 13.

Wong, Chun Han. "SlutWalk Singapore Puts Feminism in Focus." *Wall Street Journal*, December 7, 2011. https://www.wsj.com/articles/BL-SEAB-300.

World Economic Forum (WEF). "Global Gender Gap Report 2021." Accessed May 18, 2021. https://www.weforum.org/reports/global-gender-gap-report-2021.

World Policy Analysis Center. "Constitutional Equal Rights Across Gender and Sex." January, 2020. https://www.worldpolicycenter.org/sites/default/files/Fact%20Sheet%203%20-%20Constitutional%20Equal%20Rights%20Across%20Gender%20and%20Sex.pdf.

Ybarra, Michele L., Kimberly J. Mitchell, Merle Hamburger, Marie Diener-West, and Philip J. Leaf. "X-Rated Material and Perpetration of Sexually Aggressive Behavior Among Children and Adolescents: Is there a Link?" *Aggressive Behavior* 37, no. 1 (2011): 1–18.

Yeung, Wei-Jun Jean, and Centre for Family and Population Research. "Singapore Longitudinal Early Development Study Research Update Issue 2." National University of Singapore, July 2020. https://fass.nus.edu.sg/cfpr/wp-content/uploads/sites/17/2020/09/Research-Update_Issue-2_July-2020_opt.pdf.

Index

Lightning Source UK Ltd.
Milton Keynes UK
UKHW051138281221
396103UK00011B/42

9 789811 249